MURDER AT WAYSIDE ANTIQUES

ANNA FLOWERS

RAVEN PRESS
Melbourne, Florida

AUTHOR'S NOTE: All facts concerning this case have been reported accurately based on available public records and interviews. Some scenes and conversations, however, have been created for interest.

MURDER AT WAYSIDE ANTIQUES
Copyright 1999 by Anna Flowers

Please contact the publisher for written permission to reproduce any portion of this book. All rights are reserved and parts of this book may not be reproduced in any form or by any electronic or mechanical means including information storage and retrieval systems without their permission, except in the case of brief quotations embodied in critical articles and reviews.

First Edition, January 1999
Current Edition: 8 7 6 5 4 3 2 1

ISBN: 0-9666362-0-1

Published in the U.S.A. by: Raven Press, Inc.
                                   P.O. Box 410368
                                   Melbourne, Florida 32941-0368

MURDER
AT
WAYSIDE
ANTIQUES

Other books by Anna Flowers:

BLIND FURY
> The story of prolific serial killer Gerald Stano

BOUND TO DIE
> The case of Tampa serial killer Bobby Joe Long

Both published by   PINNACLE BOOKS
Kensington Publishing Corp.
New York

MURDER
AT
WAYSIDE
ANTIQUES

For Frank Alioto,

who introduced me to this story,

and for the Branum family.

1

The tall young man with dark blonde hair stood transfixed at the glittering entrance to Binion's Horseshoe Casino on Freemont Street's original Vegas Strip. A chattering midget with a seducing spiel was spinning a large Big Six wheel. He had just walked the three blocks down "Glitter Gulch" from the motel room where his pretty Mexican woman and their baby daughter slept in the cool of the desert night.

He felt as tall as Vegas Vic, the five story cowboy waving down at him. He loved this town. It was April, 1983. During the day a pawn broker on Boulder Highway had told him all about the midget, and he needed to make some new contacts. In this town he didn't fool anybody with his wholesome good looks and innocent blue eyes. He was a career criminal with a ten year record and some of that mileage showed.

Lewis called himself Gary Johnson tonight, and he hoped Lady Luck recognized him by that name. He walked into the busy club, bought chips, and continued past the crowded roulette table. Jovial drinkers and gamblers were being highly entertained by the croupier calls. "Place your bets. Place your bets, before the ball drops and the wheel stops. The wheel spins and you win. The new winner is number three! Pay red, pay odd, pay the first twelve and the first eighteen." Quickly the house paid the winners, raked the losers and spun the wheel again.

Lewis walked on by. The Big Six dealer was his interest and he hurried to one of the remaining seats to place chips on a number. The midget's darting, dark eyes quickly sized him up: Rube. With a toothy smile under his black moustache, he reached up to give the large vertical wheel another brisk spin. It clicked and groaned and came to a stop on a silver spike.

"Five. Number five pays. Number five will get you two for one," he chanted as his muscular arms, just reaching over the table, stretched to rake in all the chips but one. He was saying, "Place your bets. Hurry! I have the shortest odds in the house. Even you can beat a midget but you have to play to win." He was thinking, *welcome, suckers!*

Lewis was really getting a kick out of this guy, who, at a pudgy four feet, seemed like a carnival character. Talk around the wheel was that his name was Steve Vento, from Milwaukee. Lewis liked this round-faced little man immediately. He was obviously a veteran entertainer and probably about his own age. A pair of long legs under a short, tight leather skirt next to him made it harder to concentrate. He was tempted to just relax and enjoy, but he had a large inventory of stolen goods stashed in a personal storage warehouse that needed to be moved. It should be easy in this city where the money flowed like the Missouri River.

The midget smiled at the fresh-faced newcomer thinking he had an easy mark. "Place your bets," he grinned, and the stoic smile did not change as Lewis started to win. Obviously it was a sucker game but he played the odds by doubling his bet when he lost, and was ending up a winner. The house watched a while then the pit boss signaled for Steve to get lost. When his replacement moved in, Lewis scraped his piles of chips in a paper bucket and left the table. On the way to the cash cage, he slapped a few backs and made jokes about his good luck. The Southern drawl and the habit of lowering his head to look up to speak did make him seem like a rube, but a likeable one.

Walking out he glanced longingly at the famous one-million dollar display of one-hundred, ten-thousand dollar bills in the impenetrable plastic showcase. Security monitored it and the entire establishment from an unseen location. Outside, he saw Steve standing in the shadows, smoking. He walked up to him, took out a large roll of cash, and handed him a hundred.

"I want to give you this off the record. I know you

have to split with everybody." He smiled down at him. "I want this toke to be just for you."

"Thanks a lot," replied Steve, noticing for the first time the gap between his front teeth.

"Do you party?" asked Lewis, handsome enough to make the space between his teeth seem incidental.

"What do you think this is?" Steve asked, grinning his more perfect smile as he muffled the joint with his two small fingers. "I'll save this for later."

"Fine," said Lewis. "How about showing me around town?"

"Cool. I'm through for the night. Your treat."

They worked their way among the crowds down the six-mile Las Vegas Boulevard Strip. Huge neon signs reflected a continual garish sea of colored lights. A thirty-foot Sultan, moving dancing girls, a silver slipper and swaying palms all beckoned them to enter each club. They chose spots where good-priced drinks would include famous headline acts. Many milling about at this hour were dressed so outrageously that no attention was paid to a six foot man with a midget. Such anonymity was precious to Lewis.

Again in the car, Lewis reached under the seat and pulled out a box of jewelry. "Do you like any of these rings?" he asked.

"Certainly I do." The chubby fingers were already riffling through the box as if they were selecting candies.

"Take what you like," smiled Lewis, intentionally sealing the relationship.

Throughout the rest of the night they continued bar hopping at the casinos.

Lewis's story was that his parents owned the largest antique store in Missouri and that he went around the country buying and selling antiques for them. He told his attentive little friend that he had some beautiful stuff stashed in San Antonio where his wife's parents lived and he needed buyers for it. He gave amusing accounts about how he traveled as needed, skimmed good pieces from collections and put his share in storage around the nation. He added that he always had access to a lot of drugs.

Steve confided that he didn't know what he liked best: the drugs, sex, or acting. Professionally, he played characters, and for the past few years he had been under contract with a restaurant franchise working as a popular hamburger character.

"This is the rascal that chases Ronald McDonald around in the ads," he laughed. Even though he was only in his mid-twenties, he had been around Vegas on and off for several years dealing Blackjack, Roulette, and Big Six. "I've met all kinds of people," he confided, "and they're not all nice."

When they finally called it a night, Lewis asked, "Do you know anyone around here who might be interested in buying my stuff?"

"Just might," said the midget. "Stop by the club when you get back from your, ah, buying trip."

◆

2

It was almost morning when Lewis stopped his green station wagon in front of the midget's house on Palm Hurst Drive. He was tired but decided to drive back to storage and switch his car for the blue pickup truck being stored there. He needed the camper truck for his run to Mexico. It looked like an ordinary vacation vehicle, but he had customized it with concealed compartments for hiding drugs. There were springs on the door panels, false compartments in the headliner and floor, an extra dummy gas tank (his personal favorite), and other unique storage spaces.

He returned to his motel with the truck, entered the room quietly, and crawled into bed beside a soft figure. His baby daughter was sleeping in a crib nearby, so he whispered as he embraced the nude body of the woman. He loved how she smelled and the way she responded to him when he slowly explored her young body with his hands. He had bought the Mexican girl, called Terry, for five-hundred dollars. He bragged to many that it was the best purchase he ever made.

Terry was slim with the classic Latino features of dark hair and eyes, full face, and ready smile. She was born Soila Casias into a large family of migrant workers, and she had learned a lot about life before ever meeting Lewis. Trouble was no stranger. Through hard times or good ones, the family stuck together and tonight she was happy to be joining them in San Antonio. It would be possible to get there tomorrow in just one full day's drive from Vegas. She imagined they would leave late in the day for a cooler ride through he desert, but that would be his decision of course.

By twilight, the three were well into the desert, the baby comfortably asleep again between them on the broad front seat. Terry entertained herself with an all night Spanish speaking radio station as Lewis drove silently, mulling over the details of his job ahead.

Only twenty-five now, he had been a frustration to police for many years. He was so amiable when caught burglarizing properties or running drugs, that he did not appear to be a threat. He never resisted arrest, confident that no jail could hold him for long. Recently he had escaped confinement in Corpus Christi, Texas and had fled to avoid prosecution in Albuquerque, New Mexico. He was smart enough to know it took about two days for an FBI check on his prints, and he never gave police time to cross check his open warrants in four states.

It was an amusing game to him. This time he would go under the name of David Wayne Hendrix, he decided, because his last alias, Francis Wayne O'Connor, was wanted for stealing the truck he was driving now. He's a good old boy, too, he chuckled to himself. He thumbed through the collection of driver licenses in his wallet. One for Lewis Wesley Walker was there but he was also wanted in San Antonio and Corpus Christi for burglary and auto theft. He shuffled them like cards until David Wayne Hendrix was on top, then he put them all back in the window of his wallet.

When he finally arrived at the Mexican section of San Antonio, Lewis woke Terry to guide him through the vast area of government subsidized apartments. They were recycled World War II military barracks, and looked alike to him. Terry's mother, Julia, lived in one with her common law husband, Felix Covarrubias, and others. The truck moved slowly through the dark compound with Terry peering at each unit. Finally they came to her mother's place.

Julia was waiting in the house. Many people had come and gone during her night-long wait. She ran outside when the truck stopped, and embraced them all at once. She scooped the baby up in her arms, cooing to her in Spanish, and went inside to show her off to Felix.

Inside, a large pot of hot, dark beans was simmering on a blackened burner. They sat down around a small table in the dimly lit room, and bowls were filled. Felix passed a bottle of red wine and Julia extended her cup in a toast to her granddaughter, Christina. The flamboyant women talked rapidly in Spanish. Lewis could understand almost everything they said. Although he always spoke softly, almost childlike, when he did speak the whole family stopped to listen. They also responded in English because they had much respect for this man who always had a lot of money.

"We're going to be leaving soon for North Dakota to work sweet potatoes," Julia said later, clearing the table. "Some of the men who would normally be making the trip are in jail, including Pedro, Felix's brother." She stood near Lewis. "You do well and seem to always have the answers. Who would help us?"

"You don't want to know who helps me," Lewis smiled, looking toward the floor. Terry also often wondered where the money came from, who paid him and for what. She could only guess, and really didn't care as long as there was money.

"Wise up, Mama," she laughed, her hand habitually tossing back her long hair. "He only tells me things like: *Don't look a gift horse in the mouth*, whatever that means."

Felix, a wrinkled, worried man of few words, blurted, "We've got to find some way to get more of my people across the border, especially now that Pedro's doing time." His concern was not so much for the employment of his kin but the fact that as team boss he got an override on their pay from the farmer.

Lewis didn't answer right away although he knew he'd be in Brownsville in the morning en route to Mexico. He was a mule for Roque Garcia, a large scale drug importer and distributor. He had done just about everything but murder for the man. He transported gold belonging to Roque across the border and brought back black tar heroin and cocaine. Of course he was always paid well.

"Maybe I can help you, Felix," he said finally. "I'll be in Mexico on business in a little while. Can you make arrangements quickly?"

Felix's tough, brown face broke into a wide smile. "I was hoping you'd say that. Everything's set."

During the next few weeks, Lewis crossed the border numerous times for Roque, picking up drugs. Each time he returned there were Mexicans in the truck and dope in the compartments. Once in Brownsville the workers were on their own, and Lewis proceeded to various cities designated by Roque where buyers waited. When his last haul was completed he drove to a storage unit in San Antonio where he switched vehicles and loaded stashed jewelry for the run back to Vegas. He now had a full light brown beard and longer hair, and he was using still another name.

He drove back to Julia's to pick up his family.

"I'm glad you're not in jail," she laughed, greeting him.

"If you don't have the money, honey, you'll do the time," he responded, hugging her as he slipped a large roll of money in her hand. "This is for expenses while I was gone."

He walked over and patted Felix on the shoulder. "We're going back to Vegas now. We'll see you all soon in Dakota."

"The Scott farm in Gilbey," Julia reminded him, and waved goodbye.

◆

3

Lewis returned to Vegas with instructions to lay low until Roque contacted him again, but he was ambitious to become more than just a mule for a drug lord. Having seen the big money, he now wanted his fair share of it. This move had been planned for a long time while he learned from the best. He had much to offer.

He was no ordinary burglar, and was certainly known to be one of the most ingenious in the business. An ability to recognize valuable art objects and jewelry came from working in his mother's antique shop in Missouri. Other handy skills were developed while working in his father's junkyards there. He had a knack of seeing how things were put together and could easily take them apart as well. As a teenager, he could quickly steal and operate any kind of vehicle, including earthmoving equipment and huge trucks. Being able to cleverly improvise tools from any materials at hand was another important attribute that served him well. With a paper clip carried in his stocking he could unlock handcuffs in seconds. He delighted in demonstrating this to police. With one turn of their heads he would be handcuff-free and smiling.

His plan was simple. He would generate enough money from robberies to buy part of the drug action. He would market the best of the jewelry obtained and have the rest melted down for gold and silver, which was as good as cash in most drug deals.

Anxious to put this plan into action, Lewis stopped by the club to see Steve, who introduced him to a Keno junkie named Tim Catt.

Catt knew everybody in the jewelry business and was a hustler who never turned down an opportunity to make a buck. He sold everything from high-ticket items for Diamond Jim to single gold necklaces, requested by some of the dealers at the casino. Catt operated a small jewelry store in a strip shopping center with easy access to the shops of his sometime partner, Diamond Jim. They were both colorful characters with individual specialties.

Lewis joined Catt in the Keno parlor and took a comfortable chair, although he had no intentions of playing. In Keno, he knew that the house had an exorbitant edge of between twenty to thirty per cent depending on the odds variations in the number of selections. Unquestionably, it was a miserably unfair game and not one to risk money on, regardless of how modest the bet.

Trying to beat long odds was nothing new to Catt, who enjoyed the leisurely tempo of the game and, of course, the free drinks. The game itself, as Lewis had seen, was a random process in which a machine called a "goose" blows twenty of eighty numbered plastic balls into two transparent tubes. When each ball appears in a tube, the number is announced on the address system and also appears in lights on display boards throughout the casino. Obviously, if only twenty numbers turned up in a game, sixty did not, so the odds against a particular number coming up were three to one. The house paid only two to one.

"It's similar to bingo," Catt explained, "but you guess the numbers." Catt marked his card, numbers one through eighty, with whatever numbers fit his fancy. He took a pull on his cigarette, winked at Lewis, and signaled for a runner to take his money and ticket to the writer who would validate it. Soon a copy of the ticket, good for only the next game, was returned to him.

"Hey!" he said, by way of explanation. "It's just a little investment and I just might hit it big." Silently he concluded that Lewis was a super, super hillbilly.

"Right," replied Lewis. "It probably costs you a lot less than the slots too 'cause it sure takes longer."

Catt got to the point. "Shorty said you had some stuff you want to move."

"Yeah. Sooner the better," replied Lewis, flicking his fluffy hair from his forehead.

"Anytime," nodded the hustler. He and his pals had

their own interpretation of the phrase "honor among thieves." They used every dirty trick they knew while negotiating, but when the deal was struck, it was done. Catt wasn't taking him to raise, but Lewis already knew the ground rules.

Before Lewis left however, Catt decided to enlighten him by discussing a deal he'd made once with Jack Weinstein when they were still business partners.

"You know, a while back I had to get to Detroit quick and I needed money. The only thing I had was an old Mercedes, one of those classic models. Jack had admired it before so I asked him what he'd give me for it. He fiddled and fumed and finally offered me five grand. I took it. Later that day, with the Mercedes sitting at the curb outside, a guy comes into the store. Jack didn't know I was within ear shot, and guess what? He sold the damn thing for fifteen grand on the spot. Really pissed me off, but what could I do?"

The next day, Steve and Lewis carried several bags of jewelry to Catt's small shop in the Diamond Exchange strip shopping center. Eagerly, Catt dumped the contents onto a black cloth on the counter top and was openly surprised at the quality of the merchandise.

"From an estate sale," grinned the midget.

"From *somebody's* estate," countered Catt.

Only Lewis was serious. "Give me a good deal and there's more where this came from."

Catt pulled the magnifying glass down from his

forehead to take a closer look. A three-carat marquise cut stone in a unique setting got his special attention.

"Nice," he commented. "This is what's called a Valerie mounting. I think I might already have a buyer for this one." He looked up and winked. "She's a friend of Diamond Jim's. A little gal with a big passion, especially for diamonds."

He removed the glass and reached under the counter for a small compartmentalized briefcase. It looked like something designed for military secrets, but this metal case had rows for necklaces and slots for rings.

"This should hold them," he said, deliberately arranging the jewelry. "We'll take a look at them on Jim's machine next door to verify the quality. It's not that I doubt your assessment, but you can't be too careful in this business."

"I understand perfectly," Lewis smiled. "We'll go with you."

They walked to the adjoining shop and Catt took a look at the pieces under an expensive, specific gravity machine. This machine resembled an overhead projector with electronic numerical data displayed on the bottom. Instinctively, Lewis' blue eyes checked everything in the room: high windows, good locks, good alarms, and in the corner, a smelter.

"That's a big one," said Lewis. The midget followed Lewis' eyes and walked to the large smelter.

"Yes, it is. Jim melts a lot of his gold and silver to make new mountings or necklaces."

"A first class operation," replied Lewis, thinking that this was indeed a fine way to reprocess hot merchandise.

At that moment a curvaceous customer knocked on the locked glass and iron front door.

"That's one of Jimmy's best customers. She likes to call me "Tom,"" Catt grinned. "You two scram through my shop and I'll keep in touch." Lewis slapped his pocket for the list of contents as he dropped off the case. Steve went into his Charlie Chaplin walk as they exuberantly made their exit.

◆

4

Lewis was heady with his positive reception at the Jewelry Exchange and he was anxious to return to Texas for more merchandise. When he made a routine call to Roque, however, his plans were changed. He was told to go to Florida immediately with his family, stay within a half day's ride of Miami, and to await further instructions. His contact would be a Columbian who was putting a big drug deal together.

Roque's Texas operations center received constant updates not only on product availability but also on what different states were doing to thwart drug traffic. His source in Florida reported that a current profile for suspects included males, Hispanic or black, who traveled in pairs in fast, late model cars. Roque chose Lewis as the perfect contrast. He would be traveling with his wife and family in an older camper pickup truck. This deal was a very important one, and Lewis was definitely the man for the job.

He left Vegas promptly, took the southern Route 10 through Texas to Florida, and Interstate 75 south into Florida. The trip had been uneventful, almost monotonous. The temperature rose rapidly as they drove east even though it was only April. He was tempted to stop in Gainesville, but decided to go a little further to Micanopy where he got a cheap motel with a greasy diner.

The next morning they had breakfast there. An older waitress who looked like she'd been up all night brought them a cup of black coffee with a spoon splashed in each cup. On the table was a dusty bowl containing a few packets of sugar. You had to ask for cream.

"I hate that," frowned Lewis, removing the spoon. "Why can't they put the spoon on the table?" He knew the answer even as Terry spoke.

"I guess if they set the utensils out they would disappear."

The kitchen was not serving the advertised homemade biscuits this morning. "They're old. Order something else," advised the crusty waitress.

He ordered toast instead and eggs, over easy. When the meal came, the eggs hadn't spent enough time in the pan and they ran all over his plate. Terry's sausage looked like a hockey puck, but he thought her scrambled eggs probably a better choice. When he asked for more coffee, instead of bringing a pot to the table, the waitress gathered the mugs, overlapping her thumbs inside each one, and returned with the two steaming cups minus spoons.

"No tip, bitch," he muttered to himself as they left the diner for a reconnaissance drive. Catlike, he paced off adjacent territory. The road now had a roll to it, the first hint of hills in a thousand miles. It was lush, green countryside and along I-75 brown wooden stick fences protected sprawling horse farms. Well-groomed horses grazed underneath huge live oak trees that bent with hanging Spanish moss. An occasional palm tree or palmetto reminded him that this was Florida not Kentucky.

When they passed the Town and Country horse farm, an impressive oval training track could be seen from the road. He began to notice road signs advertising an antique shop. A stand of woods appeared on his right and he crested a hill to begin a mile grade down to exit 72: Orange Lake and Irvine. He could now see the northeast corner of a large, white, two-story building. It had four massive white columns supporting a ridged metal roof that overhung double front porches. Tall billboard pilings supported a sign that read, "Wayside Inn Antiques." The building was within just a few feet of I-75, separated from it by a wire fence. He guessed the structure to be about fifty-by-one-hundred feet. A big operation. Odd, he mused, to have such a store out in the middle of nowhere. He couldn't get the place out of his mind.

He took exit 72 left and parked across the road opposite the building and used binoculars to study the interior. Terry spread a blanket on the ground and played with the baby. Through double glass doors and four large windows he viewed an elegant shop full of attractive antique furniture and display cases. A multi-colored stained glass ceiling in the center of the main room cast a rich glow over the contents. Lewis decided that this was a world class shop, full of riches just waiting to be collected by him. Soon he calmly gathered his family and drove back to the motel, but he was too excited to sleep.

The next evening, after the shop had closed, he drove back alone and took exit 72, right. The dirt road with thick tropical growth on either side looked like a place time forgot. At a fork in the road, a wooden sign said, "Calawood RV Resort, Left." He turned right toward the antique shop and parked his truck in a thicket. An old corrugated metal barn was on the left just before a pair of white wooden entrance gates. After that, the oval road swung right and within a short distance turned left, along a barbed wire fence adjacent to the highway. Left again, it continued the oval by the building and parking lot, to the exit.

Lewis grabbed his binoculars and went as close as he could get on foot.

"What a setup," he whistled under his breath, brushing away his mop of hair to see better. It was a Butler building with overlapping metal siding, put together with screws. Routinely, he made a careful analysis of the job. Easy to get into, no dog, no bright lights. The trailer home to the north was too far away to hear or see anyone on this side. He shook his head as if it was almost too good to be true, then quietly doubled back, eased his truck onto the highway, and returned to the motel.

When he got there Terry was excited with a phone message. He immediately went to a pay phone booth outside and called Roque in Texas. He was told to be at a Miami address at noon in two days. His contact would be a man named Caesar, and he was to bring the drugs straight to San Antonio within forty-eight hours of the pick up.

"Wonderful news!" he said to Terry, shutting the door and grabbing her for a big hug. "We'll have tomorrow here and the next morning we'll leave for Miami."

"Happy days are here again," he sang, grabbing her for a little Texas stomp around the room. Although she laughed, she was thinking in terms of his clichés, sensing danger to come: waiting for the other shoe to drop.

The next day Terry, wiry and industrious, helped pack everything into the truck and they all went to bed early. During the night, Lewis slipped out of bed, pulled on his jeans and jacket and quietly gathered two cloth sacks that he had set aside. He put the sacks and a few tools and gloves into a dark bag, clasped them under his arm and walked out to the highway. Although there was not much night traffic, he soon caught a ride south. Thanking the driver, he hopped out at exit 72, and watched as the car lights disappeared.

He silently moved along the now familiar route to the building, and cautiously stopped short of the parking lot opening to pause and listen. No sound or movement except for sporadic highway traffic. He quickly crossed the open parking lot and crouched next to the building near some bushes. Moving carefully along the side, he chose a small, three-by-three-foot panel of metal siding to remove. Within seconds, he loosened the screws holding the panel and bent the metal back. He listened. No alarm. Reaching inside, he felt an interior wall which he cut and pushed in far enough to enter. Still no alarm. He forced the black bag in and squeezed in behind it.

Standing up he found himself surrounded by a wonderland of priceless antiques yet allowed himself no time to savor the scene. Quickly he moved to the center of the shop and darted behind a large, rectangular glass display case. Within moments he filled the sack with jewelry, watches and silver items, carried it to the opening, and pushed it out among the bushes. Turning back he filled the second bag with carved ivory pieces and small ornate figurines, which he thought to be valuable.

Once outside, Lewis secured the tops of the bags and took them individually, along with his tool bag, down to the fence. Then he climbed the fence and hid the bags in the brush. The entire job had taken only a few minutes.

Happily, he walked the six miles back to the motel. He jumped into his pickup truck without closing the door, put the gear in neutral, and pushed it away from the room before starting the engine. There was still little traffic when he pulled over to the shoulder of the road, went up the incline to the fence and picked up the bags hidden there. With them safely packed in the camper he returned to the motel for a few hours sleep.

Very early the next morning, they checked out of the motel and began the trip to Miami. He was relieved when he drove by the Wayside Inn Antiques that all appeared to be quiet. He flashed a gap-toothed grin at Terry as he thought of the new inventory for the Las Vegas market. But first he had to concentrate on picking up the drugs for Roque.

The pick up in Miami went routinely once Caesar, who was accustomed to dealing with high rollers in fancy cars, got over the surprise of Lewis' redneck demeanor. The plastic sacks of drugs were packed in styrofoam boxes similar to those used for carryout chicken. They were promptly packed out of sight into a compartment under the camper bed. It was business as usual. The schedules of these drops were more reliable than the airlines. Soon the nondescript camper was on its way north again with its valuable cargo.

◆

5

David and Betty Branum had not been home on the grounds the night before when Wayside Antiques was robbed. The robbery had occurred early in the night and they had left hours before that for a celebration dinner with their son, David Jr., and his family. Their son lived a few miles south in Belleville in a modest but comfortable country home which included enough land around it to keep a horse. His wife liked to ride, an interest shared by many people in the Ocala area, but Dave preferred keeping a classic truck in show condition in his spare time. The entire Branum family thoroughly enjoyed the youngsters and always made time to support their activities.

Last night there had been a school recital and the senior Branums had arrived home late. This morning Betty walked over to the shop, went in the back way and started the coffee as usual. John, the manager, had opened minutes earlier, and Catherine was already going over some paper work in the office.

"Good morning," called John as he opened the cash register under the stairs. "How did your granddaughter's program go?"

"She was great," answered Betty, flashing a big smile. At fifty-five, she was still attractive though greying. Her energy was evident in every movement in spite of a few extra pounds. Chatting about the children, she gathered a cloth to wipe the glass display case in the center of the room. She abruptly stopped her dusting and called to John, who was now in the office. "Did you do something else with the jewelry here?"

John was already bringing out the good stuff from the safe and almost dropped it when he saw the empty areas in the cases. "Good Lord, we've been robbed!" He shouted over his shoulder to Catherine, "Call the police and your Dad!"

The Marion County Sheriff's Office responded quickly and investigated the side wall entry. By the time Tom Gates got there, inventory assessment was well underway. It appeared to be only a minor loss.

Betty tried to be patient with the police questioning. Although outwardly gregarious, for the past few years she had been fighting lymph cancer. Her doctors now said her condition was in remission, but she still could not tolerate much tension. She stood quietly wishing that all these people would just go away and leave the lovely shop tranquil again.

David saw the police cars from the house. He ran over and paced back and forth, angry that he had not been home. Betty, who lovingly watched her husband, was thankful that he had been gone. She edged over and slipped her arm around him to calm him down, but he was tormented with the thought that he could have made a difference. Tall, lean and rugged in appearance, he had never been the type to walk away from adversity. He was a career Army sergeant, retired in 1972, and through all of his adult life naturally protected what was his. He was also a gentle man who preferred to settle disagreements with words, if possible.

For the past seven years he had worked for Tom Gates, principally doing repair work while Betty helped tend the shop. They left for a short time to open their own antique shop, but returned to Gates because of the job security. He was comfortable with his current arrangement. Everyone associated with Wayside seemed to look out for each other like a family.

He also appreciated the fact that his son David lived nearby with his family, and that his other son, Randy and family, lived less than a day's ride away in South Carolina. This was important to him since moving around so often in the military had all but estranged him from his relatives back in Tennessee.

In April 1946, he married Betty, a nineteen-year-old girl whom he thought was the prettiest girl in Chattanooga. They had an interesting life rearing their children in different parts of the world. The travel was educational. In Europe they learned enough about antiques to easily identify good pieces. David became especially interested in old clocks and was expert at repairing and restoring them.

He and Betty had decorated and furnished their present double-wide mobile home with good items collected over the years. Occasionally they would add another piece that Gates offered them at a special price.

Besides their home, another job benefit was David's unlimited use of the store's large workshop. In it he squirreled away all kinds of materials for his continual projects. There were yards of gold framing, for instance, in case he needed it for a picture or mirror repair. This morning he thought, *What the hell. I've saved all my life and now some jerk comes along and takes what he wants.* Although the missing things belonged to Gates, he felt a strong personal violation.

◆

6

By the time Lewis passed the antiques shop on his way back to Vegas, the Marion County Sheriff's Office had already investigated the robbery of the night before and were back at their office filing the report.

Tom Gates, the owner of the store, was walking around bewildered that the burglar had not used any window or door where there was a sensitive alarm system. Obviously, this had been done by an experienced robber, unlikely anyone from this small town. But would he return for more? His three-quarters-of-a-million dollar inventory was virtually intact. He was also puzzled that his shop tenders, David and Betty Branum, who lived on the grounds, had heard nothing.

Gates was a small, intelligent man. His many business interests took so much of his time that he left the operation of this shop to others. He did the buying, however, and took pride in the fact that the store was widely known for quality merchandise from all over the world. Just recently he found some magnificent pieces in France.

It was difficult creating displays that looked warm and inviting in this vast building, but that had been accomplished. The open expanse had a second story wrap-around balcony with colorful railings and poles from a European circus. The green and yellow poles were carved with gargoyle faces. Interesting, yet almost overpowering, the entrance contained unusual items such as a Gothic bishop's chair, an ornately carved wooden bar with a stained glass back, and, beyond that, a sixteen-thousand dollar music box.

In the center of the room were six long display cases, arranged in a thirty-by-fifteen-foot rectangle, where jewelry, antique art objects, expensive china, and watches were displayed. Above this was a suspended ceiling of stained glass that bathed the shop in a pleasant glow of reds and golds.

On either side of the store, under the balcony, antiques were arranged in open groupings by type and period. Each room contained treasures.

In the right front were three carved French oak sideboards, priced individually at ten-thousand each, four large armories, and three curio cases. This display was filled with valuable objects of china and silver plus remarkable cut glass items that shimmered in the light. Outstanding was a large bronze and silver-plated, two-foot tall ewer, or water pitcher, on an eighteen-inch platter. The base was decorated with lizards, lily pads, and frogs. A figure of a woman was on the side of the ewer handle, the spout was leaf design, and figures of men and women in relief surrounded the center. Its value: $9,500.

Adjacent to this display was a Louis XIV room, which contained two walnut sideboards, an ornate 1745 Bombe clock (offered at $13,000), a Chinese vase and stand, a rosewood chest and a fifteen-foot dining table with ten chairs. This and other adjoining period rooms were furnished with large collector's items and each of these rooms carried an approximate appraisal of $100,000.

Gates himself had bought most of this inventory and his good taste and flair for the exotic was reflected everywhere.

To the left of the store were two rooms of antique office desks, chairs, and equipment. Antique mantles held unusual art objects and valuable oil paintings decorated the walls. The administrative offices, with desks and large safes, were positioned next, followed by the sales station, which was located under freestanding, wide wooden stairs. Located here were two brass cash registers and an ample wrapping area. Shipping and receiving of larger items was done from a wooden platform at the rear of the building.

The upstairs balcony, with its gaily painted circus railing, generally contained less valuable items. An exception were four bronze chairs that sat at the top of the stairs. They were Art Nouveau classic chairs flowered seats. They dated 1890-1920 and were ten-thousand each.

Around the balcony were interesting collectibles such as a life-size wooden drugstore Indian, unusual mirrors and antique wooden airplane propeller blades.

Gates' hobby was model trains and he also developed this to outlandish proportion. In a twenty-by-forty-foot room, he created a scale transportation system in a natural setting. The handmade train models wound authoritatively through mountains, cities, along highways and past ports. There was actual water for the rivers, boats at the docks, and planes on the airfields.

On the balcony outside of this room were more trains. These were sophisticated European models, also handsomely displayed, and they were for sale.

The store was an establishment that not only offered priceless antiques and collectibles for sale, but it seemed to almost magically entertain the browser, satisfy the entrepreneur, and transport the imaginative into another time.

Tom Gates had always felt comfortable with his children involved in the business. Catherine kept the books and Martin, whose real interest was wood sculpturing, did sundry tasks. He had a family-like relationship with employees David Branum, who was good at repairs and his wife, Betty, who worked in sales. He felt fortunate also to have a knowledgeable store manager, John Sikorski, who could ably run the shop.

But at this moment, Tom felt violated by the burglary and was still puzzled that only his lesser-valued inventory had been taken. Stolen were some ivory pieces, including a chess set and some small carved figures, but overlooked nearby was a $10,000 three-foot carved elephant tusk of a Chinese woman.

All that his young manager, John Sikorski, could initially determine missing were some silver and turquoise Indian jewelry and several sets of gold cufflinks and tie tacks. Three dozen moderately-priced watches were gone from the display case as well. The valuable watches were always locked in the safes at night.

After hours of more intense inventory scrutiny was conducted, the staff found that also missing were numerous small sterling silver pieces including candlesticks, cream and sugar sets, and salt and pepper sets.

The total claim to the insurance company was $13,000. After the one-thousand-dollar deductible was met, $11,690 was paid.

◆

7

During the following weeks Lewis hurried on to other states in pinball fashion, banging a stop here, then there, covering rendezvous points miles apart. This movement would have made his apprehension difficult even if the Marion County police had been following him.

He went directly to San Antonio with Roque's Miami shipment and arrived ahead of schedule. This allowed him to touch bases with Julia and Felix and leave his wife and child with them.

When night came, he drove to a large warehouse in the industrial section of the city where he quietly parked his camper near an unmarked door. At the wall box he nervously glanced around before punching in the code. As soon as he started his motor again the metal warehouse door began to creak up. The door closed electrically behind him as he waited his turn behind a tractor trailer.

The huge warehouse had a wide traffic lane directly through the center. On either side there were large open bays where merchandise of all description was stored in truck load lots. It looked like a public warehouse where several businesses stored inventory. From a rig in front of Lewis, a forklift was off-loading some lawnmowers and yard equipment, but Lewis was signaled around the truck to a forward area where two men rushed out to accommodate him. A cocaine shipment took precedence. The biggest cash payday of Lewis' life was made on the spot. He also was given a large supply of canned food still in cartons. After that he was told to get out and get lost until he was contacted again.

On the way to the storage unit, Lewis finally began to relax. He exchanged the blue camper for a green station wagon, transferred some of the canned goods and selectively chose ivory pieces from the robbery to show Julia.

The mood in the Mexican compound was sullen when he arrived. Bad weather at the Dakota farm had delayed the migrant workers being called to the job. The result usually was heavy drinking, senseless fighting, and economic hard times. The canned goods, gratefully received and shared by Felix, made him somewhat of a hero. Julia quickly stuffed a gift of money into her undergarment.

Lying beside Terry that night, he wondered if her bed would be empty if he were not there. Though he suspected that such a passionate woman needed his constant attention, he did not know that she sometimes worked nearby bars in his absence. When morning came, he decided to make the trip north with the Mexican entourage. They would all go to Dakota but he could not stay with her long. Sooner or later he would have to continue to Las Vegas alone.

Before leaving, Lewis went by the storage unit once again and this time he emptied it. He carefully packed the jewelry and small art objects from the robbery into the false floor compartment of his station wagon. Soon the group started out in separate vehicles, caravan style, heading north on Interstate 35. Most were hungover and disheveled but all had high hopes of making money.

When they arrived at the camp, the community kitchen was cleaned and set up with some fresh supplies, the remaining canned goods, and some cooking utensils. There was an enormous feeling of comradery in this effort. The active children all played in a swarming group under no particular person's supervision, yet continuously watched by all.

Lewis did what he could to help, but once the farm work began, he was on his way to Las Vegas with his newly-acquired merchandise. Vegas always got his juices flowing and when Lewis hit town this time he was so energized that he only paused long enough to call Steve Vento to meet him at the Jewelry Exchange. As he drove past the familiar pleasure palaces he fought an urge to stop. He was growing impatient with the slow-moving traffic along Freemont Street. Working girls had been propositioning him at almost every stop light. Finally he pulled over and briefly gave one his business.

When he arrived at the Jewelry Exchange, the midget was already in Diamond Jim's store. He could see the two men in animated conversation as he passed the iron-protected glass front. He walked next door to see Tim Catt. Smiling, Catt crushed a cigarette with his fancy cowboy boot and greeted Lewis warmly. He had sold everything that Lewis left previously. Inventory lists were compared and each item was checked off. Lewis kept looking up shyly and running anxious fingers through his thick, dark blonde hair, but in the end he accepted twenty-five percent of dollar value. They shook hands and walked over to Diamond Jim's.

Jim's reputation was larger than his physique. Lewis didn't know what he expected, but this mild-mannered little man was not it. Back East a guy in this business would be a much flashier dresser and pushy to a fault. Jim wore heavy gold jewelry, of course, but his clothes were country casual. With limited conversation, he acknowledged Lewis with a limp handshake and the four men sat down at a table in the back. Vento, who had never seen the new stuff, was as surprised as the others that it was of such high quality.

Jim never asked questions when he couldn't stand to hear the answers. As a retail businessman, however, he had to make a cursory inquiry about the origin of the pieces in order to protect himself. Lewis, anticipating this maneuver, produced some bogus certificates. Vento, who was more or less just waddling around the table, was impressed. Catt, thinking of more deals to come, nervously brushed ashes off his cowboy shirt and excused himself.

Over a period of time Lewis and Jim did more business with some significant trading as well. Jim had an elegant broach with large purple stones, which Lewis admired and traded for three dozen strap watches of various makes. Jim purchased some ivory snuff bottles, nude figures, horses on stands, uniquely carved chess sets and other items for his display cases. Jim also melted down small pieces of silver items and pocket watches for which Lewis was paid $6,400. He figured the melted transaction alone financed the entire inventory.

He watched and admired the way Jim operated. Items which he thought to be legitimate, or at least untraceable, such as a twenty-seven-inch scrimshawed whale's tooth, were displayed and sold. Large unusual pieces had to be discretely placed with buyers, and a few other items like some walrus tusks remained in storage for the present.

All the players were pleased. Diamond Jim, and ultimately Catt, had a lucrative new source of jewelry and art objects. Steve Vento was amassing favors owed him by Lewis, plus getting a little kickback. Lewis also sponsored free entertainment for him on the Vegas Strip.

This new set up ended, however, with a phone call from Roque. He had an assignment for another pick up in south Florida in June. That gave Lewis time for a San Antonio run but no time to visit the family in Dakota. He worried about Terry but business came first.

The camper for the job in Florida was stored in San Antonio. Tonight he was back on the eastbound highway out of Vegas. In the monotony of the miles he would catch the beams of an occasional oncoming car and follow them until tail lights disappeared from his rear view mirror. He wondered how many of them were also carrying drugs.

He pulled off at a service station for a sandwich and coffee and took a second cup into a phone booth to call North Dakota. He was surprised to hear that Terry and the entire family had unexpectedly returned to Texas. He wondered what was going on, but in just a few hours at Julia's house he would have the answer.

He walked into the apartment and slammed the door. He saw Felix sitting drinking beer with someone. When the guy turned around, Lewis was startled at the evil in his eyes.

"This is my brother, Pedro. Remember I spoke to you about him," said Felix, greeting Lewis and handing him a beer.

Lewis nodded, visibly repulsed by the man's scarred face and emaciated condition. They were direct opposites. Pedro's piercing black eyes were empty and cold as they focused on Lewis' blue-eyed, Anglo Saxon face. Lewis concluded that prison time had not improved Pedro Covarrubias. Unlike his brother, Pedro did not smile nor offer the touch of a handshake. Instead he stared disapprovingly at Lewis, making him very uncomfortable.

This is one mean Mexican, Lewis thought. *What the hell is he doing here around my family?*

Later, sitting on the outside steps, he grilled Terry, "Has Pedro bothered you?"

"No," Terry assured him, "but you're right. He's weird. I'll be glad when he's gone."

Felix, on his way out for a smoke, overheard the conversation and shut the screened door behind him. His steely gray hair and perpetual worried look made him appear older than his years. "I think drugs have made Pete the way he is. He's always done them, but this time at LaLuna he really got into it big time. Sometimes he acts loco. I wouldn't cross him."

"What's going to happen to him now?" asked Lewis.

"That's the big question," Felix shook his head and sighed. "He doesn't fit in at the farm. He won't work and he'll cause plenty of trouble both for himself and for us."

"Why doesn't he just go back home?" Lewis said with a frown, probably guessing the answer.

"He's in trouble there too. The organization he used to run with would like to get their hands on him. You can't cross guys like that and expect them to just forget it." Lewis remembered hearing that Pedro was with the Mexican Mafia, but thankfully couldn't remember any details.

Felix flicked the remaining nub of his cigar into the darkness and turned to face Lewis squarely. He knew no other way to say it. "He wants to go with you," he blurted, "and make some of that easy money."

"No," responded Lewis firmly. "I work alone."

"I know, I know," pleaded Felix, "but please think about it. We're desperate here."

◆

8

Under family pressure, Lewis decided that taking Pedro with him was probably best for all, especially for Terry and the baby, and he might be of some help. The rest of the family returned to the farm, while Pedro and Lewis went to Florida. They didn't talk much and certainly not about the primary reason for the trip. Lewis knew that it would be foolish to let a drug addict know about the Miami pickup. He guarded that information literally with his life.

Over the miles, Lewis devised a scheme to leave Pedro at the Micanopy Motel while he went south supposedly to shop for horses for an associate. This person, he told Pedro, needed to launder some money and the Ocala area had some of the best horse flesh in the country. Pedro bought the story, but he was very bad at waiting. Lewis, however, was developing more patience with him, realizing that he would need help in stealing the larger antiques. He promised Pedro they would do the robbery on their way out of state. Even with this understood, Lewis still had to invent ways to keep Pedro busy for the next four or five days.

It was now June 21, 1984, and his instruction was to call Roque on the odd days and to check for calls at the motel desk at noon on the even days. Lewis had to do this secretly.

In the meantime, he drove Pedro to Ocala to case numerous gun and pawn shops just to amuse him. They sized up the shops that specialized in guns and jewelry. Among them were the Magnum Pawn and Gun on old Highway 301, Bargain Box Pawn and Gun on 441, and Jerry's Discount. Selecting one to possibly rob was confusing to Pedro. This was humorous to Lewis who had no intentions of robbing any of them. He could not chance getting caught on petty theft before completing the big antique burglary. Pedro wanted transportation while Lewis was gone, so when Lewis spotted an unattended motorbike he pushed it in the camper and soon it was in the motel room.

His first priority now was the antique robbery. Using the name Jerry James, he visited the beautiful shop with Pedro, who saw only dollar values that could be converted into drug money. After their first visit Pedro became even more hyper. On subsequent visits Lewis assigned him things to do. He had him locate offices, identify the shipping area in back, and spot the alarms. All useful information. This allowed Lewis to go into his carefully planned routine, browsing among the smorgasbord of delights. His plan was to select a few good pieces, bargain for them and leave a down payment. This would explain returning for them later.

Betty Branum finished using the brass cash register under the stairs and started over to help her new customer. Marty Gates, who had been watching Lewis consider some of the more expensive pieces, decided to wait on him himself.

Lewis was amazed at how much of value he had missed on the first robbery several weeks before. By shopping leisurely this time, he could make a much more intelligent selection. As Marty approached him Lewis flashed a broad grin and said ironically, "There's just so much to choose from I hardly know what to pick."

"Take all the time you need," smiled Marty in response.

"Actually, I really like this little old boy reading a book." He slowly rotated the statute noting the fine detail. He also noted the $375 price tag.

Marty saw this too. "If you would like to make an offer..." he suggested, his voice trailing off.

"How about $300?"

Marty hesitated a moment and Lewis slyly lowered his head to return the figure to the display case. "Done," said Marty brightly. "That's a very good choice. I'll set it over on the counter with Betty while you look around. Call me if you need anything."

"Thanks," replied Lewis, trailing behind him to talk to Betty. "I'd like to make a deposit on this and maybe some other things if that's alright," he suggested, almost apologetically.

"Of course. That would be fine," she said. Suddenly, Pedro appeared from the back, startling Betty.

"I'm on my way to look at some horses and I'll be back for these things in a day or so." Lewis quickly explained. "This is my groom, Pete. He'll be back with me."

Lewis continued browsing around the magnificent store identifying what he knew to be valuable, transportable, and resalable. When he bargained for items in the ten-thousand dollar class such as the bronze and silver ewer, Marty called John, the manager, into the negotiation.

"You certainly know your antiques," said John, pleasantly enough. Lewis sensed his guarded arrogance.

"My mama taught me how to spot them," Lewis replied in a deliberate country manner.

"Obviously," sniffed John, tilting his smooth chin in an effort to look close to his thirty years. Actually he looked like a handsome Mediterranean boy with dark bangs and brown eyes, an appearance he thought to be a business deficit. He tried to be sophisticated. Lewis simply thought he was overbearing.

Lewis liked Betty Branum though. She was very friendly to both he and Pedro. Chatting over coffee, he learned that she and her husband, David, lived on the grounds and were available most anytime he wanted to come back for the purchases. He gave her the deposit and signed the invoice "Jerry James."

Back at the motel, when he was finally contacted for the drug pickup in south Florida, he was ready. He left Pedro with some personal drugs, a little food money, and the motorbike.

When he arrived in Fort Lauderdale, Lewis had difficulty finding the designated address due to the one-way streets and numerous canals. When he finally pulled his camper to a stop, the transaction was made quickly. It was up to him to stash the cocaine so that police or Pedro could not find it. He had rehearsed this part well.

He already had the spare tire loose in the back of the truck. He filled it full with the sacks of cocaine and reassembled it underneath the truck bed. Then he sprayed it with a dog repellant and tossed the empty can into the weeds. He had rigged other devices before such as the extra gas tank for a load, but the tire seemed appropriate this time. More money was paid for innovative new ideas on hiding drugs than writers were paid for new jokes. Lewis thought of his own concealing places.

Carefully, Lewis drove the northern route again past Orlando through Ocala and on to Wayside Antiques, making sure that his arrival time at the shop was after working hours. Branum had another appointment however and when Lewis got there the house was dark. He pulled up and left a note saying that he would return late the following evening. He attached it to a small light by the door and went on to his motel. It had been a long day, but Pedro wanted to hear the game plan again for the robbery. Lewis kept it simple. They were to meet the Branums, gain entrance to the shop for their purchases, tie them up, and take whatever they wanted. Before sleep, Pedro showed him the handcuffs and ropes he had packed for that purpose. Things should go smoothly and they would be out of state when they slept again.

◆

9

Lewis telephoned Betty Branum as soon as he awoke and apologized for missing her the night before. He explained that the Orlando horse auction was running late and that he would meet her that evening about six o'clock. She agreed. He smiled as he hung up the phone thinking how simple this job was going to be.

Lewis had a sinking feeling when he glanced at Pedro, who was pacing the room like a caged animal. Pedro's unpredictable behavior worried him. He would be glad when this was over.

Soon he parked the truck across the highway from Wayside Antiques and waited with Pedro for the shop to close. When the last car was gone, they drove over to the Branum's mobile home and knocked on the door.

"Hello, Mrs. Branum," he smiled. She noticed the gap between Lewis' front teeth again and wondered why his parents hadn't taken care of that when he was little. Regardless, she thought it a handsome smile.

"Come in," she beamed and gestured them inside, happily expecting a huge sale. Tonight she could even tolerate his somber companion. David entered as they were being seated and he offered them iced tea. Lewis casually glanced around the well-furnished room making note of their personal antiques.

"That's a real beauty," he said, pointing to one of their prized possessions. It was a round clock, encased in a rectangular base. Rearing back on top of the clock was an unruly bronze horse with a small figure of a boy on the ground trying to control him.

"We bought that in Europe a few years ago," David said.

Pedro, who communicated little except to nod or grunt impatiently rubbed the knees of his jeans and uttered, "We'd better go."

"Right you are," said David, raising his long frame and taking out a handkerchief to wipe his glasses. "I'll help you load up if you want."

The four walked to the loading platform at the rear of the shop and David unlocked the door. He immediately turned off the alarm system. As they walked through the shipping area he pointed out the items being held for them on lay away.

Betty was still chatting amiably. "I'll get your receipts from the office. Be right back."

In the main display area, Lewis continued to impress

the Branums with his ability to identify and discuss antiques. He had collected objects from various locations in the store and set them on the counter near the cash register under the stairs. David and Betty verified the value of each item from the price sheets and a purchase price was agreed upon. They had been authorized by Tom Gates to cut the price by a certain percentage when such volume was involved.

The telephone rang by Betty's hand and she answered it. Lewis was relieved to hear it was a personal call. She cheerfully mentioned that she was in the middle of a large sale and would return the call.

Somehow the ringing phone was like an alarm for David, who suddenly became suspect of this situation. He tried to think rationally. These men had identified twenty percent of their best inventory. What seems too good to be true usually is. Yes, there was definitely something wrong here. He tried to shake the feeling, but when he studied Lewis it became chillingly clear.

Lewis sensed discovery. The comic mask dropped from his face and was replaced by cruel indifference. Pedro, whose intentions had always been suspect, came forward.

Suddenly, the room seemed to explode. David reached under the counter for a small hand gun. Pedro grabbed an antique musket from the wall and hit David, knocking the hand gun to the floor. He picked up the gun and pointed it at the couple. Betty screamed, "Please don't hurt us, take what you want!"

Lewis warned Pedro, "Don't hurt them. I'll get the truck." He ran out the back door and moved their camper closer. Breathing hard, Lewis ran back and forth loading the preselected merchandise, unable to ignore Pedro as he hit David.

"For God's sake, calm down! Don't mess it up!" he screamed at Pedro.

Betty crumpled into a pile on the stairs, sobbing. Pedro kicked her husband and demanded that he open a large green safe in the office. When David insisted that it was old and would not open, Pedro became livid. At gunpoint he shoved the pair into the office where he had seen another safe.

Lewis hoped he could finish before Pedro went berserk. He scooped up trays of jewelry from the counter and ran with them to the truck, trying to block out the crying and loud voices. Suddenly it was quiet. Pedro had taped their mouths shut. Then gun shots echoed through the shop and Lewis froze in momentary disbelief. He ran inside and braced himself at the office doorway, taking in the grisly tableau. Betty was handcuffed to a safe with her mouth taped. David, handcuffed to another safe, had been shot in the head. Pedro was rifling through the desk.

Lewis stumbled outside and vomited. His head was spinning and he could hardly stand up. He struggled to focus his mind on the task at hand, to grab as much as he could and get out of there. Instead of going back inside the store, he went to the Branum's trailer and gathered their personal treasures, including the bronze clock he had admired only a short time before.

On his way back to the truck, he saw the lights go out and Pedro appeared on the loading dock with arms full. They got in quickly without exchanging words. Lewis drove away so fast that the camper door flew open and one of the bronze chairs fell out. He stopped, ran back to retrieve it, and secured the door. Pedro got under the wheel and drove to the highway. Crossing a bridge, Pedro rolled down his window and hurled the gun into the darkness below.

"A perfect job. No witnesses, no weapons," said Pedro. For the first time that Lewis could remember, Pedro smiled.

◆

10

Marty Gates quietly eased out of bed, pulled on his jeans so as not to wake his wife, and went to the kitchen. After he made coffee he perched on a stool at the far side of the kitchen counter and drank some from a fruit jar. The sun, already intense at this early hour, heated an unlocked sliding glass door behind him and beamed on the unfinished figure of a manatee. Work on the wooden piece had been abandoned for weeks. Here in the sedate little town of Micanopy things seemed to wait until you got back to them. Everything, that is, except his pretty, petite wife who refused to be ignored at any time.

Presently she came in with tussled blonde hair wearing only his tee shirt, and she got his complete attention. He had known her since high school but just the sight of her still excited him. She giggled as he grabbed her for a kiss.

Marty was muscular and well proportioned but not

much larger than his wife, a physical characteristic that she found attractive. In the past she was often uncomfortable with male friends who loomed in size, seemingly controlling her. She considered this threatening although she did not know why. With Marty she felt equal and loved. She also admired his creative talent, undisciplined as it was. Communication between them was good, and she knew at this moment he would much rather stay home than go to work at his father's store. She guarded against the slightest encouragement that would make him stay, allowing only a lingering shower together.

By nine o'clock he arrived at the antique shop and was surprised to find the entrance door locked. Usually David Branum had already opened up and the aroma of Betty's freshly brewed coffee would be present. This morning there was only silence.

He entered and paused at the disheveled display cases, turned and froze in horror at the scene through the open office door. Blood was everywhere. Betty was slumped backward over a chair with her left arm handcuffed to a large green safe. David was leaning forward on his wife with his hands behind him handcuffed to a smaller safe. Their mouths were sealed with wide packaging tape and both had been shot in the head. They were wearing clothes that Marty remembered from the day before. The room was completely trashed with records strewn everywhere, and it reeked with the stale, sickening smell of blood. Marty did not enter.

When he was finally able to move, he mechanically

made it to a phone where the number of the Sheriff's Office was prominently posted. His throat was dry and his voice sounded like someone else's as he reported the murders. On the other end a dispatcher calmly noted the time as 9:03 and began to log details of the possible double homicide.

When he heard this, Investigator Leo Smith sighed and shifted his muscular body. He was thirty something and in good physical shape except for a bad eye he'd had since birth. Although almost blind in it, the eye did not effect his work. A graduate of Ocala High School, he knew most of the local people and he enjoyed dealing with the country rowdys. Kicking butt was his specialty, usually with a laugh about it afterwards. He was widely known as a fair and effective law officer, and he was extremely pleased with that reputation. Less known was a determined passion to progress to the top of his profession.

Leo reread details of the double murder. Ironically, even though murder was relatively rare in this county, there had been another homicide the day before involving a domestic dispute. A dead woman had been dumped on the bank of a nearby lake. Someone else would have to investigate that one. He was on his way to Wayside.

He jumped in his car, turned on the flasher, and proceeded north on I-75 at high speed. He thought a lot during the twenty-minute ride past familiar countryside. He had always lived in Marion County and was aware that the Ocala area was a contrast of people who had and those who had not. The wondrously wealthy horse farm owners seemed to be above the law. Misconduct or legal scrapes were generally resolved quietly. Known substance abuse or personal vendettas, sometimes resulting in serious reckless acts, brought only legal slaps on the wrists. The hard-working hands got paid as much for their loyalty as for their services. Leo grinned broadly as he drove, thinking that cowhands since the days of the Wild West had had fun dodging the law. He knew, however, that if he had lived during those times he would still have operated on the right side of the law. He lifted his western style sheriff's hat and ran a big sunburned hand over his dark curly hair. Yep. He was rugged enough to have been a cowboy.

 He turned on County Road 318 and made a dusty halt at the entrance gate to the antique shop. He greeted Deputy Oran Pruitt, who waved him on through, and he parked near the porch steps. He jumped out and got an update from Sgt. Jim Mahaffey and Deputy Billy Woods. When Evidence Technician Georgia Whitson arrived, she announced that a sizeable investigation team was on the way. Roaring up in rapid succession came John Rathmann, Tom Little, and Chris Blair, followed by Captains Martin Stephens and Gerald King, and, with special urgency, Sheriff Don Moreland.

 Individually, everyone was taken inside to the murder scene. The wide store aisle was configured so that each investigator could clearly see the bodies without disturbing or contaminating anything. The brutality of the murders suggested a professional execution. When the Sheriff saw this he immediately decided to call in the Florida Department of Law Enforcement. He needed their assistance and the use of their extensive crime lab. Soon Special Agent John Burton joined the investigation and two more technicians, Leroy Parker and Terrell Kingery, came with him. While these FDLE specialists were gathering information, Leo took Marty Gates aside to interview.

They sat down at a table on the porch. Marty was still visibly shaken. He slowly told Leo about the two men the Branums were to meet. He described one as Jerry James, a white male about six feet tall, one-hundred-and-sixty pounds, with brown hair. He described the other man as possibly being West Indian or Hispanic with a dark, pocked-marked complexion. He judged him to be about five-eight, a hundred-and-fifty pounds with greasy, black wavy hair, maybe in his mid-thirties.

Marty recalled that these men were to meet the Branums the night before to pick up layaways. He detailed a series of their visits and produced store invoices showing the sales items, price, tax, and down payment. He remembered that the man known as Jerry James bought statues from him on Wednesday of the preceding week and had made a cash down payment. On Sunday, James had dealt with David Branum, purchasing two vases that were put on layaway. This second invoice had listed his address as Reno, Nevada, but gave 89101, the Las Vegas zip code.

"David remembered he had a Shriner's meeting

Monday night," continued Marty, "so the second pickup was delayed until yesterday. But when I left work about 5:30, Jerry James had not been by. His vases were packed in boxes and we made out another invoice. Both invoices and the two boxes are missing, along with a leaded glass peacock that James particularly admired."

Leo was making rapid notes for his report. Marty had never seen the suspects' vehicle but the description of their appearance should be helpful. He called an investigator over to record Marty's description of the missing items for the preliminary list and to gather all the invoices. When he noticed that Marty's father had arrived, he quickly excused himself and walked over to the store owner. Tom Gates was devastated with grief. Leo put a hand on his shoulder and led him to a private spot at the far end of the porch.

"Dave and Betty were like my own relatives," Tom said tearfully, taking out a handkerchief to wipe his wire framed glasses. "Like my brother and sister. They were such caring people." He collapsed to a seated position on the wooden landing and leaned against the wall for support. Leo stood patiently on the limestone rock walkway giving the man time to light a pipe and gather his emotions.

"I think that's what got them in trouble," Tom mused between puffs. "They were too confident that people were honest like they were and it turned on them. They were the kind of people that went beyond what a person working eight to five would do. David was a good craftsman. A jack of all trades." He smiled sadly, lines forming on his receding forehead, and unknowingly delivered an epitaph: "Whatever he did, he did the best he could do."

"Can you tell me anything pertinent to the case?" asked Smith, trying to stay focused.

"When I contacted the Branums' relatives about the death, I was surprised that Betty's Aunt Thelma Hixon had talked with her at the store about seven o'clock last night."

"Wonder how she knew they'd be working?" asked Leo, wiping sweat from his broad forehead.

"The phone rings at both the house and the store. She just took the call at the store," answered Tom.

"Tell me about the phone call."

"Well, Betty told her that she and Dave were conducting a big sale, in excess of $6,500 and referred to the customers as they, indicating more than one. She seemed very happy and nothing seemed wrong at the time."

Tom stopped talking and concentrated on slowly cleaning his pipe bowl as if to transport himself away from this point in time. Leo realized the interview was over for now and went in search of FDLE's Burton, who had arrived and was now viewing the crime scene. Leo caught up with him opposite a chiming Grandfather's clock which now sounded more chilling than comforting. Systematically he thumbed through his notes and gave all of his information to Burton, who was well into absorbing the scene. He gestured toward other technicians who would help him further, and Burton checked with them as well.

The extensive surfaces and numerous objects surrounding the murders had been an investigative nightmare. Fortunately, a VCR recording with audio had been made before anything was disturbed and it would be painstakingly reviewed. A routine check for fingerprints was made along with a search for the murder weapon or any other evidence. Around three o'clock, the bodies were removed and delivered to the Medical Examiner for autopsies.

John Sikorski, the store manager who had been in Orlando both Monday and Tuesday spoke to Leo and confirmed Marty Gates' account. Marty was then summoned by Investigator Blair for help in creating composite sketches of the suspects.

Leo was thankful to find a relatively quiet corner in which to get some paperwork done. He marked, dated, and initialed a manila envelope of evidence containing the invoices of Jerry James. Then came the forms: event forms, persons forms, and stolen property forms, all completed for logging and computer entry as file data. Finally he checked his own notes and added details. Both victims had been shot in the head by a small caliber firearm. A Ruger .22 handgun belonging to Tom Gates was missing from the counter area, but a thorough search of the store and grounds had turned up nothing.

It was about six o'clock when Leo was told that the drawings of the suspects were ready. He, Tittle, and Blair were bone tired, but they got right out to the highway exchanges with the sketches. Starting at County Road 318 they covered both north and south on I-75, showing the drawings to every gas station, restaurant, and motel along the way. Most people had heard about the murders and had their own theories but could offer no real help.

"It was a professional job," said Jamie Schofield, an employee at Irving Gulf Station, which overlooked the antique store from across the highway at exit 72. "It wasn't a spur of the moment thing. Saddest part is David Branum told me recently that he was going to retire but just didn't have the nerve to tell Tom Gates."

And so it went with all the nearby businesses. Those who knew the Branums praised them, but nobody recognized the suspects in the sketches. This was going to be a tough case to solve.

◆

11

A night's rest did not make the murder puzzle any more solvable for investigators, but working conditions did improve. Yellow crime scene tapes outside had been removed when the bodies went for autopsy. The office storeroom had been cleaned and employees were back attempting to conduct business in a normal fashion.

Leo was relieved that the crowd had disappeared so that he and John Burton could get on with their jobs. The hard to control media people were no longer competing for store workers' attention. They had gotten their footage, filed their stories, and left. Three of the sheriff's deputies had been assigned to the domestic killing on Little Lake Kerr. Of the dozen law enforcement people yesterday, only Leo and John were back at Wayside. This made it easier to work effectively with Tom Gates and his employees.

The bookkeeper/secretary, who had compiled the preliminary list of stolen items, was Tom's married daughter, Catherine Pinner.

"An accurate inventory is difficult to produce," she told Leo, "because some of the inventory sheets and sales invoices are missing."

"Then just give us a ballpark figure of the loss," he suggested.

"I'd say a rough estimate would be a quarter-of-a-million in antiques and about the same amount in jewelry." John Sikorski's wife, who worked in the office with Catherine, gave the investigators a list of watches and jewelry known to be missing. She explained that when the staff audited the store sales invoices, the two after the last sale on Tuesday were missing.

"Do you think they were taken?" asked Burton.

"They could have been used by the Branums to write up the purchases for the robbers, recording the large sale that Betty spoke about on the phone Tuesday night," she replied.

"Then they were just taken as part of the robbery, I suppose," surmised Burton.

Leo looked over to the list of missing antiques.

"I see you've included some valuable antiques taken from the Branum house. Is this figure right?" he asked Catherine. "One clock was worth $20,000?"

"Yes," she said tersely, "That list is correct."

Leo took the information back to his Ocala office and transcribed it into the report. John Burton, meanwhile, was lamenting the fact that no one had recognized the computer's two suspect composite sketches. He suggested that a police artist may be able to render a better likeness. Sheriff Moreland promptly arranged for a Lake County artist, Van Melvin, to help in this effort. Melvin interviewed Marty Gates for two hours on Friday morning refining and correcting details of the original drawings.

When he was finished, the artist passed the sketches around among everyone who actually had seen the suspects. When it was agreed that the likenesses were as close as possible, Melvin returned to Lake County to photograph his work and had flyers available on Monday. Meanwhile, Leo phoned Gainesville to follow up a lead with Blair Huffman, a personal friend of the Gates family. Huffman explained that he and his wife had been in Tampa on a business trip and were returning to Gainesville on the night of the murders. When they passed Wayside Antiques about eight o'clock they were surprised to see all the lights on with several vehicles parked in the lot.

The Huffmans agreed to undergo hypnosis to see if they could recall anything more about that night. The session was immediately conducted in Gainesville by hypnotist Phil Willis. A tape of the session was made as part of the record. Under hypnosis, they described the vehicles in the parking lot. One was a blue or bluish-green full-size American-made pickup truck with a white camper top. The second was a white or cream-colored sedan.

The vehicle information was attached to the artist's

sketches, which were again taken to every antique shop, service station, restaurant and motel in the area. The media cooperated fully. Newspapers and mid-Florida television stations frequently featured the sketches and details of the murder-robbery. Scores of reports came in and each was fully investigated.

Back reviewing Wayside records, police came across two more names to investigate. George Sanders, of Fort Myers, had consignment items for sale at the shop, and much of it had been stolen. Twenty-five small pieces of his jewelry and twenty-seven small antiques were missing. Sanders checked out to be a respected business associate and not a suspect. He had no insurance but hoped that Wayside's insurance would cover his loss under a bailer/bailee provision.

The second name, Al Nowen, appeared to be more promising. Here was a man with a flamboyant lifestyle but with no obvious means of support, except as a middle man in the purchase of antiques. On his trips from Detroit he would take pictures of some of the merchandise and would have it sold when he returned for the item. Sometimes, if he was confident of a buyer, he would make a deposit on something, and pick it up later. Whatever the arrangement, he would always emerge from his Rolls Royce with his three-hundred-pound physique expensively attired. This large, gregarious man had developed a friendly relationship with the Branums. At the time of the robbery several items were being held on deposit for him. Although Nowen had visited Wayside just prior to the robbery, he had not picked up all of his merchandise.

Leo asked Tom Gates what he thought about Nowen.

"I considered him a big buyer, a person who handled a lot of transactions. He was a cash customer," he said. "I really didn't know a lot about him."

Police tried to contact Al Nowen in Detroit with no success. Since Detroit was out of their jurisdiction, the Marion County Sheriff's Office requested assistance from the FDLE and FBI. Locating Nowen for questioning would involve time.

Every lead was explored. When the loss report was supplemented to include a Jemeter, used to evaluate jewelry, investigators discovered it had been purchased from an instrument company in Sarasota, Florida. They were contacted to see if they had a serial number on their invoice. This instrument was similar to the one Tim Catt used in Las Vegas, which caught the eye of Lewis Barnes.

Someone pointed out that in the sale of unique antiques, photographs are often used in preliminary negotiations. Smith and Burton wanted to obtain some of these photographs to publicize the stolen articles. Al Nowen had used some pictures, but of course, they were unavailable. Earlier an antique magazine had planned a feature story on Wayside that had not been printed. After some deep digging in files, pictures of many of the one-of-a-kind missing items were found and detailed descriptions were written to accompany them.

These pictures were taken to antique shows, dealers, and flea markets throughout the southeast. Articles were written in antique magazines about the robbery, murders, and the missing items. This was a time-consuming effort since magazines buy their stories for future publication, and there are thousands of antique stores.

Regardless, tracing the unique missing items was considered the best way to proceed. The artist's sketches resulted in over one-hundred-fifty reported sightings. Numerous Hispanic migrant crop workers resembled one of the sketches, prompting frightened store clerks to constantly call in. Each lead was numbered and checked by MCSO, the Marion County Sheriff's Office. With each dead end the investigators realized the importance of the antique connection. A search for the antiques was definitely the best way to proceed.

Summer dragged into fall and everyone connected with the case grew more frustrated. The FBI had traced the purchase of a handgun belonging to Tom Gates to a store in Levine, Oregon. The Ruger single six revolver, serial number 122876, was entered into the computer as a stolen firearm and was another possible trace to the killers.

In early October 1984, John Burton and the FDLE staff produced a four-page special bulletin supplement with photographs and descriptions of ten of the most valuable missing antiques. These were distributed to every major law enforcement agency worldwide.

◆

12

A giant Christmas tree blinked merrily near the reception desk in the huge lobby of the new MCSO building. Already a trustee dressed in blue-and-white stripes was making his way across the sparsely furnished room to untrim and disassemble the tree. He seemed content to remove the only joyful thing present on this early January morning.

Business had been brisk at the Sheriff's Office over the holidays, but this morning the many vinyl chairs around the perimeter of the room were empty. Even the older receptionist seemed to be operating at half speed as if she too had run out of fuel during the flurry of office parties and intensified police activity of the past several weeks.

The only other person in the room was David Branum, Jr., who stood motionless near one of the many windows across the front, waiting for Leo Smith. Since David was a building code inspector, he rode around daily checking new construction, which made it convenient to stop by here often. Through the glass he studied the neighboring Marion County Jail. It was a recently completed state-of-the-art building believed to be escape proof. He prayed that whomever killed his parents would soon be in there. He lifted his ball cap impatiently and ran stubby fingers through his brown wavy hair. The cap and the way he dressed showed definite sports interest. Although he was pounds from it now, he once played football at the University of Florida, and he was still an ardent Gator fan. Usually a happy-go-lucky, likeable guy, his parents' unsolved murders had saddened and frustrated him. Peace would only return when the case was closed.

Leo Smith was also suffering from holiday fatigue as he walked under the *porte-cochère* and entered through the sturdy glass doors. He had hoped for a day devoid of cerebral taxing. He was weary of answering questions about the Branum case. The Mayor's office, the television station, and even the waitress at the coffee shop wanted to know the latest on the investigation. Besides that, he was also concerned about the details of Sheriff Moreland's announcement on forming a Task Force. Obviously it was a politically smart first-of-the-year move, but he felt slighted by the structure of it.

The last person he wanted to talk to this morning was David Branum. He managed a smile when he saw him and gestured for David to walk down the hallway to his office. Leo waited until they were seated with coffee to begin talking. Actually he was relieved to have some news to report.

"Something significant has just happened," Leo said, shuffling papers on his desk. "Sheriff Moreland has named a Task Force to the case and we'll have the best people in the field working on it. We should get some results soon."

The lines on David's forehead seemed to ease a little with a partial smile. "It's 'bout time. Who are these guys?"

"All agencies: the FBI, FDLE, and of course, us." Leo squirmed in his seat. "Steve Benigar and Larry Jerald are the lieutenants assigned with me. Sgt. Frank Alioto will be heading up the Task Force.

"Why Alioto?" asked David, sensing Leo's agitation. "You were the lead investigator right along, weren't you?"

Damn right, thought Leo, but he squared his shoulders and said aloud, "I'm sure he'll have some innovative ideas."

Frank Alioto had been a homicide detective with the NYPD for twenty-three years before retiring to Marion County. He virtually lived the life of a TV cop, fast paced and dangerous, at the 23rd precinct in New York City. This precinct had an unbelievable record of solving over ninety per cent of its murder cases and it had become a prototype for law enforcement. He worked with the legendary Thomas J. Cavanagh, Jr., who was widely known as the Velvet Whip. This nickname was for his ability to obtain confessions in a gentle, priestly manner.

When producers searched for a location for the popular Kojak television series they chose the action-packed 23rd precinct. The exploits of Cavanagh, Alioto, and others there became story lines for the series. Like the fictional detective known to millions, these men bucked the bosses to right wrongs.

Alioto, a native New Yorker, was cited many times for his work with the force. He was supported by an understanding wife, whose father had also been a career NYPD officer. Street smart and thoroughly trained, Alioto was compactly and powerfully built. His appearance was more like Lee J. Cobb than Telly Savalas. Glib and gentle, he won people's trust at all levels. Effective as he was, near the end of his career in New York City, he knew he was lucky to be alive.

Frank was ready for a change by the early 1970's when he took his family to Florida. They bought a small farm west of Ocala with enough acreage to keep a horse, and they started shopping around for one. The land was wooded and had a slight roll, which made it perfect for building a modern house with plenty of glass. After the structure was completed and the land fenced, they were delighted to find a thoroughbred mare named Lightning Highway. Marion, his wife, was an accomplished rider and she and a daughter participated in shows. Frank became active in the Florida Thoroughbred Breeders and Owners Association. The transition to retirement seemed complete as they became an integral part of this highly-social equestrian set.

Eventually, as Frank began to miss law enforcement, he quietly eased into work with the Marion County Sheriff's Office. Over a ten-year period most of his case assignments related to the more than four-hundred thoroughbred horse farms in his area. Many of the farms changed ownership frequently under questionable circumstances. During a series of investigations he proved that some farms were being used as a front to launder mob money. He uncovered insurance fraud where thoroughbreds were bought at inflated prices and killed for the insurance money. Sometimes horses of lesser value were killed for the claim.

Frank was appalled to learn that a person could kill a horse worth millions and only be charged with a misdemeanor, cruelty to animals, with a maximum punishment of one year in jail. He worked with Assistant State Attorney Jim Phillips to draft a recommended law which was quickly passed by the Florida Legislature. The new penalty for killing or maiming a registered horse or cow was up to fifteen years in prison and $10,000 fine plus restitution of twice the animal's value. This long-overdue law was popularly received by the horse industry. He felt a sense of accomplishment with this work, but when the opportunity came to be involved in homicide again he was ready.

When he agreed to head the Task Force to investigate the Wayside Antique murders, Frank was fully aware of the difficulty of his new assignment. To date there had been few leads to work with toward solving the case. The investigation of Al Nowen as a prime suspect had been shelved. He decided reopening that investigation would be a good place to start, and Nowen became the Task Force's main focus. He asked for help from FBI Agent Mike Killgallon and FDLE's John Burton, whose records showed Nowen living in the Detroit area.

Nowen was living a lavish lifestyle without apparent means of support. He drove a Rolls Royce and had lush new digs in Coral Springs, Florida. He still had items on deposit at Wayside Antiques for which he had never returned, but there was no hard evidence against him. Even his police record was sanitized with only one minor arrest. Nonetheless, he was put under surveillance.

After several weeks, Burton and Alioto were able to get an interview with Nowen. They discovered he had complex personal problems but these did not relate to the murders. He was dismissed as a serious suspect, but shortly after this meeting Al Nowen committed suicide.

During the remainder of 1985 and 1986, Task Force members continued traveling to antique shows and shops in the southeast United States distributing photos of the stolen antiques. The items were also displayed in various antique magazines which produced hundreds of leads, but nothing tangible. Nothing encouraging happened for a long time.

◆

13

Leo Smith had tried to stay focused on the Branum murders, but he was damn glad not to be in charge of the investigation. Had someone done him a favor after all, naming Alioto to head it? The case was still a dead end after three years. Friends and relatives never stopped asking questions with their hurt and resentment constantly building. David Branum, Jr. contacted him frequently.

Finally, on July 1, 1987, at about six in the evening, Smith got a surprising phone call. It was from FBI Special Agent Charles Johnson in Las Vegas.

"We're trying to confirm a possible double homicide that occurred about three years ago somewhere in Florida. A lot of antiques were stolen at the same time."

Leo was shocked. His temples throbbed as he listened.

"I had someone in my office today and they mentioned seeing some costly antiques that were probably stolen.

The person was told there was blood on them. Florida came up. I called our Tampa office and they remembered the antique brochure and gave me your number."

"I'm glad they did," Leo swallowed. "Could be our case here in Marion County that happened in June of '84. Antiques were taken after the shopkeepers were murdered. We have a complete inventory list, of course. The most valuable ones were pictured in that brochure."

"Great," roared Johnson. "Get that list to me along with the rest of it."

Leo gathered everything MCSO had on the case and hurried over to see Mike Killgallon at the FBI office. His reaction wasn't what Leo had expected. Killgallon let out a vile oath and got Johnson on the phone.

"This is Agent Mike Killgallon in Ocala. Your conversation with Detective Smith on the Branum murders is unbelievable. You already have the damn file, Johnson, and you've had it for three years."

"I'm sorry, Killgallon," he finally responded, "I'm new here. I wasn't here three years ago." Realizing that was a feeble excuse, he added, "I'll locate those files immediately."

"By the way, they were sent to your office in the first place because the zip code on Jerry James' layaway receipt was Las Vegas. You might make a note of that," he added sarcastically.

Leo found the whole exchange amusing and told Alioto about it when he saw him later. Alioto had already received confirmation from Killgallon that the Vegas source had positively identified a brass gold-plated chair and a statue of St. George and the dragon.

"We'll leave in the morning," he said to Smith.

They were booked on a flight from Orlando International Airport which took them to McCarran International at the southern end of the Vegas strip. It was mid-morning local time, Friday, July 3rd. They went directly to Johnson's office on Las Vegas Boulevard South. Anticipation had pumped them this far, but they were unprepared for the cold reception at the FBI office.

Johnson launched into a routine briefing making it very clear that this case belonged to his office now. The FBI wanted no interference. They had warrants to search the city residences of Edwin Slade at 4236 Caliente and the home of Marilyn Slade, his estranged wife, at 4082 Twain. The warrants had been obtained after a man had volunteered a statement that he'd seen the antiques in both homes. Looking at the Wayside photographs, he verified them as the antiques he had seen. Marilyn, he added, had been warned that the articles had blood on them, and were part of a double homicide in Florida.

Johnson ordered Alioto and Smith to wait in their motel room until the search was over. Both detectives vehemently objected until they were allowed to participate. Reluctantly, Johnson agreed that they could help identify the antiques but they were to stay out of the way during the search.

On the 4th of July at eight in the morning, Alioto and Smith met with ten FBI agents at their office. Johnson softened a bit and asked Alioto to give a short briefing on the case, after which they were instructed to work with Agent Johnny Smith.

Ed Slade's corner residence was a one-story condominium surrounded by a pastel cement wall. Decorative wrought iron protected the doors and windows. Alioto and Smith were relegated to wait outside the wall. When FBI agents knocked on the door and identified themselves, they could hear a voice and movement inside. No one answered their repeated loud knocking or announcements of the warrant. Johnson gave the order for a battering ram to smash the front door.

Slade looked up from his designer phone, calmly told his lawyer he had company, and hung up. After the agents stormed in, Johnny Smith gestured for the detectives to enter as well.

Slade's home was lovely, but so cluttered with splendid antiques that there was barely room to walk. As soon as Smith and Alioto were inside the foyer they could identify each stolen piece without benefit of photographs. They had studied the case for three years. They knew when each antique was made and how much it was worth. The agents, who had to do their thing first, invaded each room taking photographs and tagging all recognizable pieces. When Smith and Alioto finally were asked to help they proceeded knowledgeably from memory. Johnson began to interview Slade, who had bought a quarter-of-a-million dollar's worth of antiques for $17,500. Both detectives were ace interrogators and were livid not to have a more active role, but they kept their anger to themselves. Infuriated by the hands-off order, they hoped patience would pay off. Serving this first warrant took the FBI over three hours. With the recovered items loaded into vans, they proceeded to Marilyn Slade's house where many more antiques were confiscated. In the final tally, all of the stolen Wayside antiques were recovered except for one item, which had already been sold at auction in London.

One of the most exquisite items found in Edwin Slade's home was the large Art Nouveau-style ewer and platter, valued at $9,500. Another significant piece was a silver-and-bronze statue of St. George and the Dragon, one of the most costly, valued at $35,000. It was thirty-inches tall and twenty-four inches long and sat on a handsome, heavy marble base. The solid silver figures of St. George on his horse with a maiden sitting beside him were depicted walking over a slain bronze dragon.

The rooms were laden with such items as a small ivory clock, eight-inches tall with a figure of a man on top. It had beveled glass windows on each side and an intriguing lower front under-dial drawer. The face of the clock was painted porcelain with figures and Roman numerals. The case was encrusted with semiprecious stones and had two unique gargoyles on the top sides. Its value was $10,000.

An $18,000 statue of Napoleon Bonaparte on horseback stood sixteen-inches tall in another room. The horse was artfully carved in ivory and wore a silver saddle. The figure of Bonaparte was silver with ivory face and hands and his right hand held the reins of his horse. The statue was on a green marble base with silver overlay decoration and the letter "N" in the center of a wreath.

Also among the outstanding antiques recovered from Slade was a light blue Chinese *cloisonné* horse, which was about one-foot tall and valued at $7,000. The saddle and blanket was of a brass-enameled, oriental design and could be removed. One of the two Art Nouveau bronze chairs with the gold-plated leaf design was also found there. The other matching claw-footed chair was recovered from Marilyn Slade's house. Each of these chairs was valued at $10,000.

Marilyn had many more of the treasures, including the colorful double leaded-glass window of a peacock that Lewis so admired. A perfect Tiffany glass lamp shade original was found in her office along with priceless statues of horses and Buddha and Chinese figures.

Smith and Alioto were experiencing mixed feelings about recent events. They were happy to have found the antiques, but they were still angry with the double shuffle. The FBI was dictating the complete agenda. Slade admitted paying $17,500 for over $250,000 worth of antiques, but he could not be connected to the homicides. Therefore, the FBI had decided to grant him immunity immediately. Perplexing.

They knew that Johnson had given them a short version of Slade's statement but they kept reviewing their information to date.

Slade had stated that on August 1, 1984, a Mr.

Bergman had informed him that some people at the local Jewelry Exchange had some unusual antiques for sale. Slade was interested and met a young man there named Gary Johnson, who showed him some samples. Slade liked what he saw and arranged to see the rest at a motel room. Slade bought them all and put the antiques in a rented storage room.

True, the FBI had located the antiques. They had, however, isolated the detectives and were not sharing information. Smith had observed that some of the fragile pieces were wrapped in 1984 Milwaukee newspapers, but no mention had been made of that. Smith and Alioto decided they needed to talk directly to the witnesses.

On Sunday they contacted LVPD Homicide Division and found a sympathetic ally. Friction between the local and federal authorities was unfortunately too common. Det. Tom Dillard agreed to help the Marion County officers investigate their case in Las Vegas.

Monday morning, July 6th, they went to the FBI and requested that the confiscated antiques be moved from the Federal building to LVPD. The reason given was lack of security for storage at the federal facility. Surprisingly, the FBI agreed. Now, with Tom Dillard's help, Smith and Alioto could begin conducting their own interviews. Alioto called Ocala and requested an Assistant State Attorney to join them. He wanted to make sure that everything was done by the book, so that evidence gathered would be admissible in court. One of their brightest young lawyers, Ric Ridgway, a wholesome boy-next-door type, was picked to join the team. Ken Engle, the Sheriff's public relations man in Ocala, was busy getting all this information to the media along with details on the antiques being found. David Branum, Jr. was being interviewed regularly, and although encouraged, he still anxiously awaited an arrest.

When they went downstairs in the Federal building, Smith and Alioto walked into the cafeteria to meet Ed Slade and his attorney. During their talk, Slade fixed the antique purchase date at August 4, 1984, since that was the date on his storage rental agreement. He talked freely about the episode, quickly glancing at his lawyer sometimes for approval, although they had obviously discussed everything in advance.

"Of course there were others involved in the purchase," he said. "One was Jeff Bergman, who owns Jem's Source. Jim Baum, too. You've probably heard of him as Diamond Jim. He owns a shop by that name in the Diamond Exchange Strip Center on East Sahara. I remember Jack Weinstein's son being involved too, but I can't think of his first name."

Slade recalled that prior to his contact with him, Gary already had sold a large quantity of jewelry through the exchange and from a local motel room.

"Could you tell us anything about what he was driving around town? Things like that would help us identify him," inquired Alioto.

"Well, his car was dirty and I think it had Nevada plates. He had two or three hand guns in the back and he was towing his stuff around in a little trailer."

"What about the situation at the motel? I know he had the antiques there for you to see. Was he alone?" asked Smith, feeling like he was extracting teeth.

"No, indeed," replied Slade. "He had a really mean looking dude with him. I mean he was scary. He didn't say a word but his black eyes were always on you."

"Can you give us a better description of him?" persisted Smith.

"He was skinny and sickly looking with real black hair. He didn't say a word even when he helped us load the antiques, but I'm sure he understood English."

"Did you do any other business with Gary other than this big purchase?" Alioto wanted to know.

Slade thought a minute, looked at his lawyer, and finally said, "Yeah. I did buy some silver and some gold rings from him once. I sold them to a local guy named Mike Laitz."

The interview concluded and the detectives went back to Johnson's office. The only other name the FBI had in connection with the suspect was Timothy Catt, a white male who was supposedly an associate of Diamond Jim. They would add his name to Tom Dillard's interview list.

Meanwhile, the FBI was working on a possible link between the Wayside murders and a set of execution style murders in California and Las Vegas. This happened in 1985 and involved robbery of some valuable articles. Actually the victims were named Tifton, but the case was nicknamed the "Ninja Murders" because the killers wore black during the executions. In this Las Vegas triple murder case, Tim Catt had been a witness for the state. The FBI thought there may be a connection.

Smith and Alioto felt more comfortable in Tom Dillard's office. They settled in across the room from each other splitting five large volumes of the Tifton murder case. Late that afternoon, July 7th, they stopped by Diamond Jim's Jewelry store.

Jim Baum greeted them defensively. It upset him when strangers popped in asking questions. These men looked like cops to him, especially the taller one, but he'd had lots of practice giving short answers.

Leo smiled down on him and identified himself and Frank as officers. "We'd appreciate discussing one of your customers if you'll give us a few minutes," he said as politely as possible. "You'll have to think back a little bit. His name is Gary Johnson."

Jim nodded, walked behind the counter and neatly crushed a cigarette in a large ashtray. He perched on a counter stool but left the detectives standing on the other side.

"Oh yeah, I remember him. It was about April '84 when he came swinging in here with another little guy, a midget I think. They made a comical pair with him being so tall. He was very presentable looking, though, and I would have taken 'em for entertainers or something. But I knew Tim Catt had been buying jewelry from him and that he had other stuff for sale as well."

"How did you know that?" asked Leo.

"At one point I saw a large silver bowl and other antiques piled in his U-Haul. The door was open."

Alioto leaned forward. "What kind of car was pulling the trailer?"

"I think it was a '77 T-bird, chocolate brown with Ohio Plates." He added with a sour smile, "I notice these things."

"Did you help Gary sell these antiques?"

Jim hesitated but decided to tell them a little more, hoping to exclude himself from what was undoubtedly a stolen property charge. "Tim and Jeff Bergman got the deal together to introduce Gary to Ed Slade. Bergman told me this."

"Did you personally do business with Gary?"

"I agreed to be his jewelry representative," Jim admitted with a sigh.

"Alright. Tell us about the midget you mentioned."

"He said he was from Milwaukee and was the Hamburgler man in the McDonalds food commercials."

"I'm not familiar with that," said Alioto. "What did he look like?"

"Dark hair, square features, heavy set, small moustache and about four-feet tall."

"Now tell us about Gary," Alioto suggested, grabbing a stool of his own.

"He first came around about six to eight weeks before the antique sale. I probably saw him four or five times. he said his father owned wrecking yards in Missouri, just across the Nebraska line. Said he also owned cattle. Gary lived in motels here. The last time I saw him was about a year-and-a-half ago. I told him not to come around here anymore because I heard his merchandise was dirty."

"Anything else?"

Jim thought a minute. "I did have some phone calls charged to me early last year. They were to somewhere in Texas. I think Gary made them."

Smith produced a piece of paper. "Would you mind signing this consent to search so we can trace those phone numbers?"

What the hell, thought Jim as he signed the form.

"Now," said Alioto, "would you tell us about the dirty antiques. How did you learn about that and what did you mean?"

"I was about to report a minor disturbance to the police one day. Tim Catt laughed at me and advised me to forget it. Said it was nothing. He told me there had been two murders over the antiques, and that *was* something. After Ed and Marilyn Slade split up I told her to get rid of the stuff, that two people had been kilt over them in Florida." He rubbed his forehead, tired of talking. "That's all I know about Gary Barnes."

"Barnes?" they both said at the same time.

"Yeah," said Diamond Jim. "I think that was his real name, Gary Barnes."

Walking next door, the detectives agreed that the new name would be helpful. They would have LVPD run off the entire list of Gary's aliases tomorrow.

There was nothing but jewelry stores in the strip mall,

and they opened the door to Jeffery Bergman's. He owned Interport and Gem's Source. As soon as they began an interview with Bergman he told them that he started his businesses in the summer of 1984.

"Tim Catt was manager of Diamond Jim's then. During the summer I saw numerous antiques at Jim's including paintings, a nice clock and a bowl. Tim Catt was there with a young man named Gary and an overweight dwarf."

"What about Ed Slade?" asked Alioto.

"Ed's an old friend of the family and he's always been actively involved with antiques. I introduced Ed to Gary and on at least one occasion they met alone in my office."

"Did you hold any money for Ed Slade in the transactions?" asked Leo.

"No. I don't even know the purchase price. Nothing." Bergman shook his head emphatically.

"Nothing?" Alioto's glare bore into him.

"Well, about a year ago Slade was at my parents' house. He told us that after the purchase he heard the antiques from Gary were stolen. Of course Gary had given him a bill of sale and all that."

"What can you remember about Gary?"

"He had a country accent from the South, and he was a smooth talker. He drove some kind of white vehicle with a make-shift trailer behind it that looked homemade. That's all I know."

They thanked Bergman for his time and left the Jewelry Exchange complex. It was twilight and the desert was beginning to cool, making it a pleasant drive to the airport. Ric Ridgway was arriving and they were anxious to update him. Things had been going well and tonight it seemed easier to tolerate each other.

◆

14

When Smith and Alioto arrived at Tom Dillard's office on Wednesday, July 8th, he was on the phone with Tim Catt. Catt was talking from somewhere in the Midwest and when Tom finished, he handed the phone to Alioto.

"Can you fly out here on Friday and talk with us? My office in Florida will send you the ticket."

Tim Catt agreed to come to Vegas but before he hung up, Alioto needed to know if he knew the whereabouts of the midget.

"Sure," replied Catt. "He deals at Binion's Horseshoe, or used to."

"That's very convenient," laughed Alioto. "We're staying across the street."

Leo was relieved to check it out by himself so in the afternoon he put on a fresh shirt and walked over to the Horseshoe. The boss, Bobby Fletcher, had time to talk and a security guard ushered Leo into his fancy office.

"Whew," whistled Leo, looking around as he settled into a deep green leather chair. "You guys sure know how to operate."

Fletcher smiled and offered a Cuban cigar, which Leo refused.

"How can I help you?" he asked, walking around his sizeable desk to another plush leather chair.

"Do you have a dwarf guy working for you here?" Leo got to the point.

"Not now, but I did. I remember most of my employees who stay a while. The little guy was a good dealer."

"Remember his name?"

"I'm not as good with names as I am with faces," Fletcher grinned. "Names change, faces don't. Wait a minute," he paused. "I think I remember him buying a house from another employee — Marty, I think." He leaned forward and pressed the intercom. "Is Marty Griffin around? O.K. Get her on the phone then."

The girl told Leo that her sister had sold her house to Steve and his brother, but she couldn't remember the last name. The address was 615 Palm Hurst and her sister's name was Ester Shaw.

Leo thanked Fletcher and later that day he, Alioto and Ridgway visited the county records office. There Ridgway used his legal skills to quickly trace the property from its current owner to Michael T. Vento. Vento had made the purchase from Ester Shaw.

In a computer search of casino employees at LVPD, Michael T. Vento turned out to be 5'9" and about two-hundred pounds. Other Vento names were searched. When *Steven* Vento came up from the same address and was revealed to be 4'4", one-hundred-thirty pounds, the Marion County team knew they had identified their pudgy midget. Michael's address in Milwaukee, Wisconsin was also given.

A check with Milwaukee Police Department Det. Donald Vomegolski, confirmed that both Michael and Steve held current Wisconsin drivers licenses, but Steve's had been suspended. They got an address for Steve and asked Vomegolski not to contact the Ventos. They could get prints easily since LVPD maintains photographs and fingerprints of all casino employees.

When they entered the name Gary Johnson into the computer they found nothing, but the name Gary Barnes gave them eight entries, all with various middle names and ages. They requested photos for pick up at eleven the next morning. Next, they followed up on information given by Diamond Jim regarding a salvage yard owned by Gary Barnes' father. Five junkyards were located in St. Joseph, Trenton, Maryville, Bethany, and Kansas City. None proved to be the correct one. They were surprised at how many people named Barnes were in the junkyard business in Missouri, but Leo, especially, was getting sick of dead ends.

When the Marion County team checked with their home office they were dumbfounded to hear that FBI agent Tom Micodemus had released a "Ninja Murders" story to the *Ocala Star Banner*. The newspaper article, printed that morning, highlighted the FBI efforts in California, the antique recovery in Las Vegas, and stated case similarities. Both Smith and Alioto were disgusted that they had not been consulted, but they considered themselves forewarned. The FBI had released speculative, unsubstantiated information which would undoubtedly put the team in a defensive position at home.

They believed that Ed Slade had been written off prematurely and that the "Ninja Murders" had no proven connection to their investigation. Alioto talked Leo into remaining silent for the time being.

The next day, with the help of Tom Dillard, all antique evidence was removed from the federal building and placed in the LVPD evidence room. Each item was tagged and logged on an inventory sheet. Included was the July 19, 1984 Milwaukee newspaper wrappings.

On the evening of July 9th, Alioto had Jim Baum review a photo lineup. He positively identified Steve Vento as the midget who had accompanied Gary Barnes.

On July 10th, the seventh day of their Vegas investigation, Leo got the phone records from Baum and called the Texas numbers attributed to Gary Barnes.

The investigators knew they had the right scent, but so far, tracks of the suspect had been cleverly disguised. When Alioto learned that Tim Catt had arrived and was on his way over to LVPD, he was energized again in the hopes that Catt would reveal something new. Catt swung into the station with bravado more befitting a party than a police interview. The cocky little man initiated more of a monologue than a routine question and answer session.

"In April to June of 1984, I was working for Jack Weinstein, who was making jewelry. In July, I met a man named Gary, through a midget everybody called the Hamburgler. Gary wanted gold and silver melted down saying he worked flea markets in the Vegas area. Shortly after the first meeting, Gary showed up at Diamond Jim's with a large silver bowl and wanted it melted down. I told him it was too big to melt. One time he brought in an ivory clock. I asked him where he got this shit and he told me I didn't want to know. I asked why anyway and he said there was blood on them. Later he mentioned these things were out of Florida. About this time he was pulling a U-Haul trailer. Once I helped him load antiques in his car after he'd had them at Jim's."

The detectives knew most of what he was saying here so they interrupted to ask for further description of Gary.

"He looked like the actor, Gary Busey, in *The Buddy Holly Story*." Catt smiled thin-lipped over imperfect teeth in an improper assumption that present were the last few people in America who remembered that film. "Gary was in his twenties, about five-foot-ten. He had brown hair, buckish teeth, and an Alabama or Georgia accent. He also told me once that he had a good-looking wife."

Alioto asked what he knew about the antique deal and Catt replied, "I wasn't any way involved in the sale and wasn't there when it went down. Jeff Bergman told me he had someone who dealt in antiques who might buy them. The introduction to Gary was Bergman's baby."

"What do you know about any jewelry associated with Gary?" the detective persisted.

"Look, I haven't seen Gary since July '84. Then I believe he had some old wristwatches."

When Alioto, Smith and Ridgway returned from lunch, Tom Dillard had news. Marilyn Slade had called asking that they pick up another antique which had been overlooked in her home. They immediately jumped into a car with Dillard, who knew the way.

Marilyn, once a real looker, opened the door with a fair amount of charm still obvious. Her perfume and jewelry were both expensive. "This is Scott Korkosz." She gestured to the man standing beside her. "He's the one who tipped the FBI."

The men sat attentively in the beautifully appointed room as Korkosz related his role in the antique recovery.

"Marilyn and I owned a mortgage business together. Sunfed Mortgage," he began. "On June 26, 1987, the County Business Regulation Office issued a cease and desist order closing us down. The person who served the order had an attorney's card with him. It was from Ed Slade's attorney. Since I felt Ed Slade was behind the complaint and closure, on June 29th I contacted George Topliapti of the FBI. I learned about the antiques and a possible double homicide connection from Marilyn on the night we were closed down."

The four men listening formed their individual images of what was being unsaid here: a personal vendetta, a love triangle, betrayal, revenge. It really didn't matter why, but knowing how the FBI was tipped was another piece of the puzzle. They thanked Marilyn for calling, accepted the handsome bronze statue of two dogs as recovered evidence, and left.

That evening, the Florida group again interviewed Jim Baum at LVPD, this time taping the entire conversation as evidence. He repeated his earlier remarks but added a few new details.

"Gary advised me up front that two people had been killed over those antiques. He said he ran dope out of Mexico and that he owed people money in New Orleans." Baum squared his chair but was unusually talkative as if he wanted to get this all out and be done with it. "He also said that people were watching him all the time, that he was the one who goes in and sets things up and later fences the property. He stressed that he was *not* the one who does the killings."

When this was over, Leo Smith squared his broad shoulders, called the Milwaukee Police Department and told them that he, Alioto, and Ridgway would be up the next day, July 11th. It was time to locate Steve Vento.

◆

15

Just before departing for Milwaukee there was a message from Ed Slade. He had finally located the merchandise receipts from Gary Johnson. The detectives and Ridgway roared up to Slade's house at 7:00 a.m., collected the receipts and continued straight to the airport.

Sitting on the back seat they looked over what Slade had given them. "Some of these sheets look like the original Wayside ledgers," commented Smith. "Where do you think he got them?"

"Like a bolt I guess he just remembered hiding them in a wall," chuckled Alioto. "You know, like behind drywall or something. Maybe where a pipe came through."

"Strange storage place," Ridgway mused, "and a cautious man."

"Just covering his ass," laughed Smith and then snapped his fingers remembering something important.

"By the way, I have a goodbye message from our *friends* at the FBI. They stopped by about midnight last night."

"Jesus," hissed Alioto. "What now?"

"They said for us not to forget whose town we'd been in."

Fat chance of forgetting their jurisdictional strong-arm tactics, thought the trio, looking down on Vegas from the plane. The morning light and the distance made it look new and beautiful. They also knew that if Tom Dillard had his way they'd be back.

They landed at Mitchell Airport early afternoon and were met by Milwaukee Police Det. David Sliquinski. He whisked them downtown using the Lake Freeway along Lake Michigan. Lt. Bob Bogle was waiting at the office with some interesting news. Steve Vento had a cousin, also named Steve Vento, who was with the police force. They contacted him and arranged to meet Officer Vento at the station at eight the next morning.

Sunday morning, July 12th, Ridgway, Smith, and Alioto piled into an unmarked car as Vento drove them to his grandmother's house.

Her older home was comfortable, very clean, and smelled of delightful Greek baking. The confident, neatly dressed woman who opened the door was obviously in charge of more than her kitchen. Steve kissed his grandmother on each cheek and whispered something quietly in her ear. She looked past his shoulder and her dark eyes assessed the strangers in her doorway. They were shown into the living room and seated. She excused herself immediately and made two guarded telephone calls. When she entered the living room again, she announced that Steve and Michael Vento and their attorney would meet with them now at a nearby restaurant.

The controlled event was staged like an old movie. The decor of the ethnic neighborhood restaurant/tavern was timeless. The large plate glass front windows had curtains across the bottom half. A cash register sat on a display case near the door where last minute smokes could be obtained when paying the bill. About three dozen square tables with checkered cloths and mismatched chairs were arranged in rows.

Along the entire length of the facing wall was a faded mural of mountains by the sea, which depicted any number of Mediterranean areas. A bar along the far wall hid the kitchen from view.

There were no other customers. The tables had been assigned for this meeting like a boxing ring. At a table in a far corner, the Ventos waited with their lawyer. Alioto stared at Vento with a withering intensity from the moment he entered the room, and never took his eyes from the midget. Ridgway, Smith, and Alioto were directed to sit diagonally to them. Officer Vento was escorted to a table in another corner where a fellow officer was already seated. Ridgway was motioned to join their attorney at the remaining neutral corner table to discuss the ground rules for the interview. He walked with confident long strides to that corner and when he shook the attorney's soft hand, Ridgway stood head and shoulders above him.

Before responding to a question, Steve Vento would be signaled by his attorney, who would nod yes or shake his head no. With a yes nod, Steve would answer, but when a no was indicated another question would be posed. There would be absolutely no record of the meeting either taped or written. Within these bounds it was difficult for the investigators to conduct an effective interview, but some general information was acquired.

The midget first met Gary in April 1983. He was staying at a Triple A motel three blocks east of Binion's Horseshoe where Steve was working. Gary lived in a ninety-dollar-per-week efficiency with his Mexican woman whom he admittedly bought for five-hundred dollars. Gary had family in Missouri and his wealthy parents dealt with horses and antiques, and he always carried a bundle of cash.

Steve described Gary as being twice as tall has he was, in his mid-twenties, with a stocky build, wide eyes and a redneck accent. At this time, Gary had reddish blonde hair and a red beard.

Steve recalled that in March 1985, Gary was driving a silver Toronado with Texas tags. He knew that Gary's in-laws were from San Antonio and that he had two children, a daughter, five, and a son, two. He said that Gary went to Brownsville regularly and that he would occasionally call him collect from Texas. When he returned calls to San Antonio, a woman speaking little English would always answer the phone.

While in Vegas, Gary dealt regularly with several pawn

shops. One mentioned was Henderson Pawn, located on Boulder Highway. But he would always recover articles pawned. Steve helped him get a Nevada drivers license using the name Gary, but the Mexican woman always called him Lewis. The woman told him that Gary had been in jail in 1984 in Corpus Christi. She didn't know the charge but knew a bond had been set at one-thousand dollars. She also spoke of Gary having a brother.

In September 1985, the FBI came to Steve's home on Palm Hurst asking about Gary Barnes involving an incident in Arizona. They also had pictures of him.

"I'm a law-abiding citizen." Steve put a small hand over his heart and rolled his eyes. "It's even make-believe stealing those hamburgers in the commercial." The detectives knew they were being conned and the meter was running. "One time in April 1985," Steve continued the charade, "Gary was at my home here trying to sell me forty pounds of marijuana. It weighed almost as much as me. What could I do but call the FBI?"

When Alioto showed him a picture of the large silver urn and asked if he'd ever seen it, his lawyer nodded.

"Yeah, I know that piece. Gary brought it to Baum's but it was too big to melt down. Gary bragged about that job in Florida when he and another guy stole jewelry and antiques and stuff. He said they handcuffed and robbed two people but they let them go."

It didn't go unnoticed that Steve was the first person to mention specifics of the Florida robbery. The detectives considered this bizarre interview a success.

Finally Frank passed Steve the line-up photo of him from LVPD. "Now that I've met you, I'd like you to sign this for me," he said.

Steve was flattered and began to sign. "Don't sign that," his lawyer warned. "He just wants a sample of your signature." He gave his lawyer an incredulous look as if he was interrupting a performance and signed the picture:

> Good Luck, Frank. The Hamburgler.

Stories about Barnes from various sources began to mesh. With each interview more was learned about Jerry James, or Gary Johnson, or Gary Barnes, or Lewis Barnes. He was emerging as an amiable thief, clever and well organized, who operated in a wide area of the United States and Mexico. He would be difficult to catch and hard to hold.

At that moment Lewis was acting like a man without a care in the world, highjacking loaded tractor trailers from highway truck stops in Houston, Texas.

On July 13th, the three travel-weary investigators returned to Ocala. After two fast-paced weeks, filled with the antiques recovery among a cast of Damon Runyan characters, they knew they were definitely on the trail of the killers.

They kept in close contact with Tom Dillard, reporting the Milwaukee meeting and checking on the evidence stored with LVPD. They wanted to make sure that the FBI had left the antiques alone.

A drivers license check on Gary Barnes produced results. Dillard reported that a Gary Dean Barnes was issued a Nevada license on March 19, 1984, which showed a date of birth of March 29, 1960, address 1020 Freemont Street, Unit 40, Las Vegas, Nevada. His social security number was listed as 495-80-6971, height 5'11", weight 175 pounds, brown hair and blue eyes. There had been no citations issued.

When the name Gary Dean Barnes was entered into the computer criminal search file, the printer literally erupted, printing page after page of data. There were sixteen names in all with variations of personal identification. The one name, Lewis Wesley Barnes, had numerous outstanding warrants and charges. At last they new the real name of the suspect.

◆

16

Alioto was hopeful that among the long list of aliases and open charges, his Task Force would find a solid lead on the whereabouts of Lewis Wesley Barnes. He had been tenaciously charting a timeline of events all along, and that was proving to be very helpful as the geography of the case expanded.

A chart was the only way to keep the cast of characters and their activities in order. Jerry James in Florida became Gary Johnson in Las Vegas; Lewis Wesley Barnes in Albuquerque and Denton County, Texas; Lewis Johnson in Cooke County, Texas; Gary D. Barnes in Brownsville and Lewis W. Barnes in Fayette, Missouri. His most frequently used names, according to arrest records, were his real name, then Lewis Gary Barnes in Missouri, Lewis Wesley Walker in Texas, with Gary Johnson the moniker of choice everywhere else. Unrelated names used by him were David Wesley Hendrix and Francis Wayne O'Connor.

The suspect's rap sheet included two forgeries, one receiving stolen property, two unauthorized use of vehicle and six burglaries in the early years. These were followed by auto theft, two unlawful possession of weapons, five larcenies including livestock, assault with a motor vehicle, aggravated assault and three unlawful flight to avoid prosecution charges in 1983, 1984, and 1985. This official record did not include the majority of his robberies or numerous drug transactions where he was never caught or charged. Several warrants did mention the use of a 1976 Ford pickup, two tone blue, license number 5009JA, expiring in 1989.

The Task Force spent hundreds of hours contacting law enforcement officials in other states concerning these charges. They continued to learn more about him.

"Man, I know the whole family," boomed Lt. Jim Gholson of Boonville PD, Cooper County, Missouri. "The person you are looking for is Lewis Wesley Barnes. He has a brother named Gary Dean Barnes, born March 29, 1960, who lives at 709 Krohn Street in Boonville. Lewis uses that name some."

"Have you seen this guy lately?" Smith asked the obvious.

"Actually, Lewis was reported to be in Sedalia, Missouri, recently." Trying to be thorough, Gholson added, "That's in Pettis County, you know."

"What else do you know about Barnes?" asked Smith.

"I know warrants have been issued in Fayette, Howard County, Missouri in reference to the theft of antiques."

"Got any more on that?" Smith prodded.

"I understand he used a U-Haul to move the stuff someplace else to sell them. He's no dummy, for sure. He has the whole thing planned like a military operation. An enforcer vehicle follows Lewis and if the U-Haul is stopped by a police officer, the car pulls up along side and shoots him."

"You're saying that Lewis is the thief but not the shooter, right?" clarified Smith.

"Right. Three-and-a-half years ago the FBI raided his daddy's place. He owns a wrecker and salvage yard in New Franklin. They missed Lewis and they didn't get anything from the brother or the parents. They all despise the law. Actually, I think the parents are involved too."

"Thanks, Gholson, keep in touch."

Leo called Sheriff Randy Yeager of Howard County, Missouri. That county is just across the Missouri River from Boonville and included the cities of New Franklin and Fayette. Sheriff Yeager had also heard that Lewis Barnes was recently in Sedalia, and added that he was a new father.

"Lewis' father's name is Johnny Barnes and his brother is Gary," reported Yeager, expanding on the family tree.

"Tell me about the brother," explored Smith.

"Well, he drives a Corvette and a motorcycle. He goes to Texas, Florida, and Oklahoma a lot."

"Why's that, you think?" asked Smith, already knowing the answer.

"Drug dealing," was the anticipated reply.

"Could you give me some help getting Johnny Barnes' phone records?" asked Smith.

"Go through Howard County Prosecutor Gary Sprick," offered Yeager, giving him the phone number.

Smith thought he might as well hit Pettis County too, so he called the Sheriff's Office in Sedalia and told them Yeager would be sending over a picture of Lewis Barnes.

About this time, totally unexpectedly, Special FBI Agent Joe Dushek called from Las Vegas.

"I've been on vacation for the last two weeks," he explained, "and I just learned you are looking for Gary Barnes. I have a whole case file and photos of him."

Fine, but what game do I have to play to get it, thought Smith.

Dushek continued innocently, "I'll give my files to Tom Dillard. I know you've been working with him."

"Thanks," managed a surprised Smith. "We appreciate the FBI's help." He hung up and said aloud, "Where were you when your bastard buddies were working us over?"

When on a roll, don't stop, he concluded as he dialed Special Agent Paul Hasselbod at the San Antonio FBI office. Hasselbod was familiar with Gary Barnes as a result of a February 1987 arrest. He knew that Gary's mother-in-law lived in the city and that his wife's real name was Soila Casias, born July 16, 1963, now known as Terry Casias. He said she had two children by Barnes.

The name he was using when arrested was Francis Wayne O'Connor.

A car seen in Missouri at Johnny Barnes' house was registered to a Paula Rodriguez of Ingleside, Texas. Francis Wayne O'Connor gave an Ingleside address when he was arrested. The FBI was checking to see if there was a connection.

The Corpus Christi Police Department and the Neucis County Sheriff's Department had four of the sixteen Barnes aliases on arrest charges. Investigation revealed that only one case fit his race and age. They agreed to send photographs, prints, and a case report for that arrest.

Detective Perez of the Cameron County Sheriff's Office in Brownsville had numerous warrants for Gary Barnes. After he had been arrested for aggravated assault with a motor vehicle in February 1985 he jumped bond. Perez too would forward what he had.

By the end of the week the Task Force reached Missouri prosecutor, Gary Sprick, of Howard County. Sprick had new knowledge of the Barnes family. He said Lewis Barnes had an ex-wife named Donna who lived in Brownsville. Barnes, he added, was a well-known thief but not a violent man, and he would always confess once he was captured for a crime.

A call from Southwestern Bell, Kansas City, said they would not honor a Florida subpoena for records. After a series of conversations, Sprick agreed to issue a subpoena for the business and home telephones of Johnny Barnes to include 1986 to present. Lewis reportedly called home a lot.

The Texas Sheriff's Department in Denton County and in Cook County also promised photographs and arrest reports.

The first week back in Ocala had been busy and productive.

On Monday, July 20th, Sheriff Randy Yeager called again to report that a bartender in Columbia, Missouri had seen Barnes in the Silver Bullet Bar about a month ago.

Smith and Alioto spent an entire week trying to track Barnes by phone sources. Sgt. John Gordan of the Missouri Highway Patrol called to say that the car with Texas tags was still at Johnny Barnes' house.

They were fed up with long distance detecting. This was as close as they had ever been to the elusive Lewis Wesley Barnes and they were not about to screw it up. They needed to be there. Hell, it was only a thousand miles away. In the morning they were on their way to Missouri to do their tracking first hand.

Smith and Alioto flew to St. Louis and drove to Columbia. They arrived at the Boone County Sheriff's Office early on July 30th, and began working with Capt. Bill McNear and Lt. Larry McCray.

A few days later a call was made from the home phone of Johnny Barnes and was connected for over fifty minutes to the residence of Dennis Harris in Freemont, California. A call was placed immediately to the Freemont PD, who gave them pertinent data on Dennis Jay Harris. He was a white male, born December 3, 1963, 5'7", 160 pounds. Caution was advised. They gave his address, arrest records, and forwarded a photo. He was not Lewis Wesley Barnes.

As the days turned up nothing new, Leo wondered why he had come at all. The FBI in Columbia had two years of open investigation on Barnes. The same was true of their offices in Albuquerque, Las Vegas, San Antonio, Milwaukee, Ocala, and other cities. What made Frank think they could do better? Still, he didn't want to miss it if there was a break in the case.

Frank was marching to a different drummer. It may not be here and now, but he would catch Barnes. He could smell it, feel it, and was dedicated to it. He would check out things here, although it didn't look promising, and just get on with it.

They rode around with Terry Mills in his Highway Patrol car from Columbia to New Franklin. Leo was bored with the redundancy of the effort. Nothing checked out positively.

Upon their return to Ocala, August 1st, Leo sent a photo package to the Freemont, California PD, tying up loose ends. The police were asked to check Dennis Harris' neighborhood in an attempt to find leads to Lewis or Terry Barnes.

Tom Dillard called Frank from Las Vegas. His photo line-up of Lewis Wesley Barnes had been successful. Diamond Jim and Edwin Slade had identified him as their business associate. He was also identified by Larry Ferguson, his old landlord, who owned a motel and casino on Freemont Street. Dushek had a guest registration card from the King Albert Motel where Barnes had billed some phone numbers. Dillard got a warrant and ran a check on all toll calls made in the February 27 to March 6, 1985, time frame.

When the March 3, 1987 traffic citation, issued to Francis O'Conner in San Antonio was received, parts of it were not legible. Leo clarified that with traffic court, then checked with Walter Winkle at Ingleside, Texas PD. He said FBI agents from Corpus Christi had been inquiring about O'Conner. Leo called the FBI there but hit another wall. An Agent Weis had been working on the case but was currently on extended leave to be married.

Leo followed up with prosecutor Gary Sprick to subpoena records of toll calls from the home and business of Johnny Barnes, and from the home of Gary Barnes. Southwestern Bell's security division gave them records from April 1984 to August 1987.

Alioto was sure that some of the grunt work would pay off, and it did. When calls from Gary Barnes' home were reviewed many were to the Olivier Hotel in New Orleans. Frank remembered that Diamond Jim had mentioned New Orleans in his statement about Barnes. Maybe there was a connection. He decided to visit the Olivier Hotel. This time Smith did not join him.

◆

17

Detective Norman McCord gave Alioto a generous smile that radiated Cajun charm and said, "Welcome to N'Awlins." His desk was one of many positioned in the huge open expanse of the old building. The police had occupied this spot on Royal Street in the French Quarter for decades as an integral and accepted part of the outrageous lifestyles that whirled around it. The big warehouse-type front windows soared high into arches with numerous separately-framed, smaller windows dropping at least twenty feet to the floor. The ceiling consisted of old hammered tin squares that were very attractive, but they leaked. A wrought iron railing had been added for a second-story effect around the room. The main floor remained as originally built, an unpartitioned great room.

McCord was as dark and handsome as a movie star.

He enhanced this appearance with fine grooming and well-tailored clothes. Listening intently as Alioto explained why he was there, he promised to help him.

"I know da French kwatas like da back of my hand. I be hoppy to show you 'round."

"I particularly want to visit the Olivier Hotel and talk to the owners," explained Alioto. "My suspect may have made some calls there."

"Olivier House is walkin' distance, but we ride first time. Fine folks there."

As they walked the brick pavement to the car, Alioto heard a trolley car chattering nearby. It was a nostalgic sound, one he had not heard in years. McCord had left the windows down in his dilapidated patrol car thinking that expected afternoon showers couldn't worsen its condition. It was quite a contrast to his own neat appearance. He laughed when he sensed Alioto's revulsion, and explained that these cars were Highway Patrol cast offs. The police commission did not have money for new cars. No matter. Old but running well seemed appropriate for this city.

Jim and Katheryn Danner had bought the Olivier House Hotel on Toulouse Street in the early 1970's and had done a great job renovating it. The rambling townhouse had been built in 1836 for Marianne Bienvenue Olivier, widow of a wealthy planter, for her family. This included fifty grandchildren. The Danners had preserved the casual ambiance of the grand old home and their own grandchildren now wandered around in the parlor and around the swimming pool. The tropical courtyard remained lush and crumbly, deliberately unmanicured. Alioto could see it from the lobby. Each of the forty-two rooms and suites had a different decor ranging from antique to modern lofts.

Katheryn Danner was calm and hospitable as she greeted the detectives although she was aware that they were from the Homicide Division. She escorted them to a room decorated with antiques and seated them near a lovely carved armoire. To Alioto's pleasant surprise, his orange velvet-seat chair was very comfortable.

"We'll get right to da point," said McCord, as he smiled engagingly at Mrs. Danner. "Dis is Sgt. Frank Alioto."

"I'm with the Marion County Sheriff's Office, as I told you on the phone," he said. "I'm here on a double murder case that happened in June 1984, near Ocala, Florida. An antique shop was robbed at that time and the shopkeepers, a man and his wife, were murdered."

Mrs. Danner's eyes widened as she heard the details of the case. "That's a very sad thing, but why are you talking to me about it?"

"We have a strong suspect from New Franklin, Missouri, named Lewis Wesley Barnes," Alioto replied, looking deeply into her eyes as he leaned forward in his chair.

"We used to live there," she acknowledged. "My son, Michael, went to school with Gary Barnes."

"Gary is the suspect's brother, and a number of collect

calls were made from the Barnes house to this hotel. We have a record of them. That's why I wanted to talk to you."

Jim Danner appeared in the doorway. "I imagine it's our son, Michael, that you want to speak with," he told the men as he walked over to put a reassuring hand on his wife's shoulder. "I'll get him, honey. You just visit a minute." He walked out and asked a staff member to send in some thick chicory-laced coffee and beignets.

Soon Michael Danner came in with athletic strides to join the group. After introductions and passing pleasantries, Alioto took out a Barnes family photo and passed it to him. "Do you know who these people are?" he asked.

"Yes," Michael replied, tapping the picture. "I've known Gary here since high school in Missouri. I've only seen him a couple of times though since '81."

"Can you remember the last time you saw him?" Alioto asked.

"I stayed at his dad's house in '84," Michael replied nervously.

"Good. That's one of the things I wanted to talk to you about. Did you make any collect calls to this hotel at that time?"

"Yes, I'm sure I did call my parents. Come to think of it, I called some friends in the city as well. Why? Is Gary in trouble?"

"Michael, would you look at this again?" Alioto extended the photo. "Do you know Gary's brother Lewis?

He's the one we are really interested in."

He shook his head and handed the photo back. "No, not really. Gary was ashamed of him. Everybody knew he was a troublemaker and a thief."

McCord sat savoring his coffee thinking that perhaps Mrs. Danner was about to hear things she may not want to hear. He was such a good detective because he noticed things that people didn't say in words. She was silent, listening apprehensively. He scanned the furnishings. "Pretty rum, Mrs. Danner," he said enthusiastically, breaking the tension.

"Would you please tell me anything else you remember about Gary?" Alioto returned doggedly to his task.

"After that visit up there, Gary called me in September to say that he was coming to N'Awlins. He drove up in an old Caddy and told me he'd sold the Corvette."

"Did he seem disturbed?" inquired Alioto.

"Right," said Michael, remembering. "He needed somebody to talk to for sure. I think he was doing a little drugs then. He had a lot of money, $3,500 or more, and asked me to go to Lima, Peru with him."

"Did you go?"

"Yes. We got our passports renewed and left from Miami. We were supposed to stay in Peru for a month." He turned to his mother who was studying her empty cup. "Mom, you remember that time." She nodded and he continued. "Gary was spending money like there was no end to it."

"Did he mention where his brother was then?"

"I believe he said he was in Mexico. Anyway, three or four days after we got to Peru, Gary abruptly announced that we were going home. He never told me what happened or what he was involved in. I haven't seen him since."

"Do you think Gary's problems could have been drug related?" Frank wanted to confirm the obvious.

"Yes, I do," answered Michael. "Gary spoke of getting help at a clinic when he got home."

"What else did he say about his brother?"

"He mentioned that his wife had just had a baby, he was an uncle now, things like that. He never gave any details about what Lewis did. I doubt he knew that much himself. Lewis was always on the move and was apparently always in some sort of trouble."

Alioto shook hands with Michael as he rose. "Thanks so much for your help. By the way, if you do talk to any of the Barnes family please don't mention this visit."

Michael nodded, but Mrs. Danner interrupted. "After you called to see me, I did speak with Mr. Barnes in Missouri." She glanced at her son. "I'm sorry, but I thought you or Gary may be in some sort of trouble."

"I'm glad you told me that," Alioto said calmly. "What did Mr. Barnes tell you?"

"He said that Gary was home and was okay. He remembered Michael from school days. I asked about Lewis just to see if he had a son by that name. He said Lewis was the black sheep and was seldom home. We just talked. I didn't actually mention that you were coming here."

"Thanks for that," Alioto said to her as he turned to leave.

McCord rose, brushed a wrinkle from his trousers and buttoned his jacket. "You've bin more than kind," he said to Mrs. Danner, who returned his warm smile.

Riding back they cut over to Bourbon Street, discussing the visit. McCord agreed that the Danners probably had no firm relationship with the Barnes family. He paused at the first corner as some sounds from a blusey guitar floated in on the aroma of spicy foods.

"No bettah," he laughed, pulling over to get something to eat. People were standing around inside the sandwich/grocery store just to savor the smells that drifted out of their kitchen.

"I'll have what you're having," smiled Alioto, knowing he couldn't go wrong.

"Two muffulettas, please," said McCord to the man behind the counter. Soon they were feasting on huge sandwiches stuffed with ham and cheese, topped with a delicious olive mixture.

After even a glimpse of this intoxicating city, it was difficult for Alioto to force himself to work. At the station, he called all the local toll numbers on the Barnes phone list. Everyone called knew Michael Danner, but none knew Gary or Lewis Barnes. He found a quiet niche and sat alone for some time reviewing his notes.

He had combed Las Vegas, Milwaukee, and Missouri,

but nobody had seen Lewis lately. Sheriff Yeager had said Lewis was a Mama's boy and called her often. There had been many collect calls from various places in Texas. His wife's family lived in San Antonio and his most recent violations were in that state. Elementary. That was where Lewis had to be: the Lone Star state.

Alioto returned to Ocala and convinced Sheriff Moreland to send him to Texas soon.

◆

18

Texas Ranger Charles Von Allen was the head of narcotics and as such did not routinely pull surveillance on warehouses, and absolutely never on Sunday. Tonight, however, a long-cooperative effort with the South Houston Police was winding down, and he wasn't about to miss the action when it came. They strongly suspected the warehouse to be a principle distribution center for marijuana, but they had to catch them in the act of transporting it to make the charges stick.

Just after midnight, September 17th, an automatic door groaned up and an unmarked new tractor trailer pulled out. Sgt. Cliff O'Quinn, stationed in the nearest patrol car with his female partner, was alerted by radio to follow. As the rig turned onto College Avenue, the officers were told to stop the driver for questioning. They followed until the tractor trailer geared down for a red light. O'Quinn hit the siren and flashers as he roared up alongside. Instantly, the driver accelerated through the light, weaving and gaining speed, erratically switching lanes. After several blocks the truck driver abruptly turned off the multi-lane road onto a side street. O'Quinn's shaven head was wet with sweat. His partner drew her weapon as he verified that other patrol cars were closing in from different directions. The truck cut its lights. Projecting through the darkness, O'Quinn could see that the street had ended in a turn-around. A narrow dirt road seemed to continue through the woods and into a field. He screeched to a sideways halt, barely missing the trailer. The driver had managed to stop his rig, jump out and run into the dark field. More cars arrived with lights blazing to join the hunt, but the suspect had completely disappeared.

The surveillance team had noticed a blue pickup in the warehouse parking lot, had traced the tag number, and now had a South Houston address. The nearest patrol car was quickly dispatched. Just as they turned the corner of the long residential block, a blue pickup truck bolted out of the driveway. The officer hit his rotating red lights and mashed the accelerator into a high speed chase. The streets were fortunately clear at this early hour as their speed exceeded one-hundred miles an hour. He drove expertly but the officers stuck with him. They could see his head turning and bobbing frantically. Suddenly, he lowered the truck window and fired a nine millimeter submachine gun at the officers. They screeched along behind him, returning the fire until the truck entered Old Galveston

Highway. Now they had him.

They radioed O'Quinn to block that road and soon the truck ran directly toward the waiting police officers. The chase car hit the brakes and the officers braced for impact, but at the last second, the truck swerved and jumped a roadside grassy strip. It bounced down an incline and landed on a frontage road leading to Broadway Boulevard. The police bounced right behind him and continued the pursuit to the area where Gulf Freeway crosses Broadway. There the pickup ran out of gas and the suspect jumped out and fled on foot. Yelling, with weapons drawn, the officers ran to the open door and were dumbstruck to see a terrified woman crouched down on the front seat clutching two small children. Other officers leaped out of their cars and ran after the driver, who had trapped himself in a fenced truck yard. Panting for breath and unarmed, he quietly surrendered.

After his arrest, he was booked for attempted capital murder of a police officer, and said his name was Victor Phillips. No bail was possible on this charge. Two days later, the police learned that they had hit the jackpot. The suspect's name was actually Lewis Wesley Barnes, wanted on numerous federal, state, and local warrants. During the routine follow-up nationally on these warrants, Sheriff Yeager was called in Missouri. Yeager couldn't wait to call Alioto.

◆

The Wayside Inn Antique shop shortly after the robbery and double homicide. The shop sits prominently off I-75 on the crest of the hill just north of the Interstate's Irvine exit.

Tom Gates, owner of the shop and Gainesville resident, sadly talks about his association with the slain couple.

The victims, shopkeepers Betty and David Branum, were widely admired and efficient at their jobs, but they were too trusting.

One of two Art Nouveau classic-style bronze chairs with gold-plated leaf design, 1890-1920. Value: $20,000 each.

Napoleon on horseback in silver saddle in the back is worth $18,000. In the center the ivory clock with precious stones is worth $10,000. All other recovered items were of similar value.

Many of the $500,000 worth of stolen antiques. Milwaukee newspaper (upper left) wrapped some. Forward right is a carved ivory elephant tusk of a Chinese woman worth $10,000. Center front is a bronze/silver compote with a gold wild boar, value $8,000.

Det. Leo Smith entering the house of Edwin Slade at 4326 Caliente, Las Vegas, where Slade stored antiques purchased from the Florida robbery.

Det. Frank Alioto, Marion County (FL) Sheriff's Office, headed the task force for the capture of Barnes. He tracked Barnes for three years.

MURDER AT WAYSIDE ANTIQUES   125

Answering media questions upon their return from Las Vegas gathering evidence are (l-r) Ric Ridgway, Florida State's Attorney's Office, and Detectives Frank Alioto and Leo Smith, MCSO.

Barnes' appearance changed remarkably. MCSO booking photo on left. Right in a photo used on "America's Most Wanted" TV show.

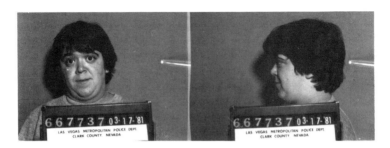

Employment file photo of Steve Vento, also known as "the Hamburglar," taken for his casino job in Las Vegas. Always the showman, during his interrogation in Milwaukee he autographed it for Det. Alioto.

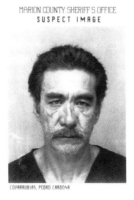

Pedro Covarrubias was with Barnes the fatal night of the robbery and, according to testimony, was the shooter.

MURDER AT WAYSIDE ANTIQUES

Barnes, after his initial apprehension in Texas, is interrogated in the Harris County Jail by Florida Detective Frank Alioto and Texas Ranger Stan Oldham.

The jailhouse window through which Barnes fled the new, "escape-proof" Marion County Jail. He patiently pried out a steel ventilator, disguising it for days with a bath towel.

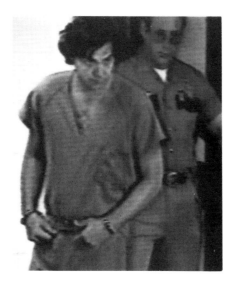

Wesley Barnes, with Detective Leo Smith, upon his recapture and booking at Marion County Jail.

Holding their daughter, Solia Casias weds Barnes in administrative offices at Marion County Jail. Alioto arranged the marriage.

19

September mornings in Ocala were beginning to have a slight nip in the air, a hint of the ideal weather to come. Alioto hummed a tune as he drove east to work into the morning sun. He enjoyed riding the road from his ranch along the wooden fences, occasionally seeing a horse's head raised in idle curiosity. He wondered why these fence planks were not painted black as in Kentucky. His thoughts wandered from that to the usual pondering of Lewis Wesley Barnes and how to find him. Texas seemed to be the state and San Antonio was looking more like the area to begin the search.

At the office, Sheriff Randy Yeager called before Frank's second cup of coffee. Yeager briefly shucked his Midwestern reserve to eagerly update Alioto.

"Lewis Barnes was arrested three days ago in

Houston," he said excitedly, "and he's being held in the Harris County Jail."

"That's wonderful news," Alioto replied, falling back into his chair.

"The best part is that he won't be getting out," continued Yeager, "because he shot at Texas Rangers. You know that's one act they don't take kindly to in Texas."

Alioto promptly shared the good news with Sheriff Moreland's Task Force, and arrangements were made for he and Smith to fly out that evening. When Ric Ridgway heard the news, he juggled his schedule in order to join them the next day. Meanwhile, to save valuable time, Ridgway flew them in a private plane to Tampa Airport.

By 8:00 a.m. Tuesday, Smith and Alioto were at the Texas Ranger Department of Public Safety Office. Stan Oldham briefed them on their way to Harris County jail to interview Barnes. The jail gave new meaning to the term "crowded." The designated interview room was part of the line-up viewing area where suspects stood behind glass. It was a long, narrow room about four-by-twelve feet with one door. The three men were large but tried to make it work. Entering the room, Alioto and Oldham took nearby chairs as Smith positioned himself at the other end by a filing cabinet. They had long awaited this moment and could care less about the lack of space. The unobtrusive prisoner was brought in and seated near the door, certainly posing no threat to anyone. He wore a white prison jump suit and leather sandals, and stared at the floor. Placing his handcuffed wrists gently on his lap, he crossed his long legs in a lackadaisical manner.

Ranger Oldham spoke first giving only the names of the detectives and himself. He told Barnes that he was being questioned about his attempted murder of police officers. Barnes was obviously frightened and when he spoke it was so softly the men could barely hear. Oldham told him to speak up, that this was serious, but Barnes already knew that. He repeatedly said he would tell them anything they wanted to know. Slowly and thoroughly, Oldham went over the entire episode including the chase, the gun battle and the arrest. Alioto and Smith listened closely as Barnes talked about stealing tractor trailer loads of goods on the interstate highways. He said he was a master thief in a ring of thieves. He gave Oldham the locations of warehouses full of stolen property not previously known. He was willing to reveal any names or places if it would help him. Oldham continued his interview through early afternoon. When Oldham was finished, he went outside and stood by the door behind Barnes.

Alioto introduced himself and Smith again. "We're from the Marion County Sheriff's Office in Florida, Lewis, and we want to talk to you about something that happened there. This is about the murders."

Alioto had Lewis' complete attention. He stared intently as Alioto continued.

"We have been looking for you for a long time. We know all about it, even who bought the antiques."

Barnes lowered his eyes and tears rolled down his cheeks. Alioto wanted to convince him that he knew Barnes had done it and only needed to verify some facts. The technique worked, and Barnes started talking nonstop, beginning with the April 1984 burglary.

"I was going to south Florida to do a drug deal with a Cuban guy in Miami. I was running real low on money. I seen this antique store up in a field and I stopped. We stopped, my wife and kids, and I went back up to where this store was and I looked it over. That night I broke into it. I took a piece of tin out of the side wall. I slipped in and I took everything from the glass cages on the inside of the middle of the building. There was a bunch of glass cages and I took all of the silver and stuff they had in them cages. Then I filled up another bag of small, little small antiques and ivory and other precious little things. I hurried out real quick and took it all back to the road and I rushed down to get my pickup. It's several miles down to where I had to walk and nobody gave me a ride. I got the pickup, drove back to pick up the bags. Then I go back and pick up my wife and we head towards San Antonio to North Dakota because that's where her mother was staying. That's where we went."

At this point, Smith and Alioto exchanged puzzled looks. Neither had heard of this first robbery in April. Alioto signaled Smith at the far end of the room to turn on the tape recorder. The recorder had been placed behind a briefcase which was on top of the filing cabinet, out of Barnes' view. Both investigators thought seeing the recorder would inhibit the confession.

"When they saw what I got and heard how much was there," Barnes continued, "they decided to come back and do the job again."

"Who are they?"

"Felix Covarrubias is Terry's father and Pedro is his brother."

"Terry is your wife?"

"Yes. Felix lives with her mother, Julia."

"I have the names straight now. Please continue. The three of you were coming to Florida..."

"We drove down in two vehicles, my pickup and Pedro's Mustang. We stayed at a motel north of the antiques store on the same side of the road. We visited the store and watched the people come and go from under an oak tree in a field north of the store. After a couple of days I got tired of waiting and left. I went to South Florida, did my drug deal, and left. When I came back, they were gone. When I caught up with them, they were home in Texas."

"So they, Felix and Pedro, completed the second burglary without you?"

"Yes, sir," he lied.

The Marion County portion of the interrogation had lasted over two hours. Ric Ridgway had arrived and they decided they would continue later. The prisoner was then led back to his cell. The men went to another room and called Ocala to talk about the April burglary. All of Barnes' facts checked out concerning method of entry, merchandise stolen, and other descriptions.

They also learned that Felix and Pedro Covarrubias, the two men implicated by Barnes, were also incarcerated in Texas. Pedro was in federal prison in El Paso, on the other side of the state. Felix was being detained in Huntsville, about a hundred miles north of Houston. Being the closest, they decided to visit Felix the next day.

Felix was brought in to the interrogation room in Ellis Unit number one. Alioto made introductions, read him his rights, and started the tape recorder.

"We want to know about you and Pedro and Lewis in Florida."

Felix's weathered face expressed surprise. "I'm sorry, but I don't even know what you're talking about."

"We're talking about the summer of '84, June and July of 1984."

"I've never been in the state of Florida," he said firmly. "During the summer of '84 I was working on a potato farm in Gilby, North Dakota. I was digging potatoes with my family. Check with them." His voice was now an excited pitch. "They will tell you."

Alioto excused himself for a moment to talk privately with Smith and Ridgway. They all agreed that Felix was probably being truthful and his alibi would be easy to verify. The interview was concluded.

Driving back to Houston, they discussed the obvious problem with Lewis Barnes' story, based on what Felix had said. Two men were reported in the store and in Las

Vegas. No one ever saw or heard of a third or fourth person involved.

South Houston Police got busy after the Barnes interview and located several warehouses containing stolen property. The Florida team thought that they might benefit from another talk with Barnes.

"There is something wrong with your story," Alioto confronted Barnes. "Felix is telling us that he's never been to Florida and doesn't know what we're talking about. We believe him."

"Why don't you tell us what *really* happened during that second robbery?" persuaded Smith.

In his second rambling version of the robbery and double homicide, Barnes described himself as the get-away driver, placing himself at the scene instead of out of state.

"I'm outside in the truck and Felix and Pedro went in, and I heard some shots and then they came out. They came running to the truck with satchels of jewelry. One of them was full of blood. There was blood all over the place."

"What about the antiques?" Alioto asked.

"We took them to Texas and rented a storage room in San Antonio," he continued giving directions and street names to the storage facility.

After this second interview, Smith and Ridgway agreed that this bullshit artist was working them over. They were not fooled by the big baby act and decided that there might be better results with one interrogator.

Obviously unhappy with the progress so far, Smith said

confidently, "I'm as sensitive as any interviewer. I can rub knees, talk with them, cry with them. Hey, look. Let me go in alone to talk to him."

Alioto strongly disagreed with Smith's proposal, feeling that he could disprove the lies and build on facts. He had deliberately begun a process for finding out what really happened. Ridgway held a middle ground as interrogation techniques were not his specialty, but agreed with Smith for a one-on-one interview with Barnes. After his interview with Barnes, Leo failed to discover any new facts, but he had succeeded in alienating himself still further from Alioto.

◆

20

Disagreement concerning procedure while interviewing the suspect left Smith, Ridgway, and Alioto a tight-lipped trio during their next day's ride to San Antonio. Putting personal problems aside, their investigation began at SAPD where more data on Pedro Covarrubias was gathered. The police knew him well. They supplied photos and a long rap sheet involving drug-related arrests along with numerous other minor crimes.

Their detectives offered to help them find the local storage facility which Barnes had described in detail. Even with his directions this was not a simple task since Barnes had used so many different names. The two most likely rental warehouses promised to search their 1984 records under all the aliases and get back to SAPD. Smith rolled his eyes, doubting that they would. Alioto sensed an I-told-you-so attitude.

By mid-afternoon, the three investigators were aboard a milk run flight to Fargo, North Dakota. The route was almost due north through the wheat belt between the Rocky Mountains and Mississippi River basin. Although it flew over beautiful farm land, the flight stopped frequently and it took seven-and-a-half hours. It followed the Interstate 35-29 route, which was the same path taken by the Mexican migrant workers on their way to Gilby. Fortunately, by the time they got there, the trio was too exhausted for conversation and retired immediately.

The next morning, Friday, September 25th, Captain Fender of the Grand Forks County Sheriff's Office agreed to escort the group to the farm of John Scott, Jr., in Gilby. During the thirty mile ride west and north to the farm, Alioto explained their goals to Fender. Locating the Ford Mustang belonging to Pedro Covarrubias was number one. Barnes said Pedro had driven it from the murder scene and that there was blood all over it. He also stated that it had been abandoned at the Scott farm. Secondly, they wanted to check the June and July 1984 employment records for Felix, Pedro, and Lewis Barnes.

It softened their own personal misunderstandings to be so warmly greeted at the Scott farm. As Easterners, it was difficult for them to visualize a 5,000-plus-acre farm. Scott explained that a section is six-hundred-forty acres and covers one square mile. He proudly added that his farm covered eight square miles. He introduced them to Kay Knorr, his bookkeeper, who maintained employment records. She agreed to search for the payroll receipts while they located the Mustang.

They bounced along in Scott's jeep through undergrowth over one of the few uncultivated areas of the farm. There among the weeds was a Mustang bearing an expired Texas tag. It was registered to Pedro Covarrubias. Alioto and Smith felt as if they'd struck gold. Captain Fender had the car towed and asked their forensics expert to scrutinize it for blood or hair evidence.

Back at the office, Kay Knorr had located the requested records. She produced copies of pay checks to Felix for work periods in June and July of 1984. All had been endorsed and cashed locally. One check had actually been cashed the same day of the murders. This was not the case for Pedro or Lewis Barnes, who had not been working during this time period. The farm managers all knew these men and their families and verified that neither Pedro nor Lewis were there at that time.

This information provided still another flaw in Lewis Barnes' second version of the Wayside robbery/murders. Felix had not been present. In the second confession, Barnes had also indicated that Steve Vento had met Pedro and could identify him. There was also the unexplained matter of the Milwaukee newspapers.

Since they were near Milwaukee anyway, they decided to go there and interview Steve Vento again. They needed to check that portion of Barnes' story, and now that he was in custody, perhaps Vento would speak more freely.

Monday, at the Milwaukee Police Department, they were met by David Sliwinski. In previous calls no one knew Vento's whereabouts, but when they contacted Vento's lawyer, a telephone interview was arranged. They asked whether Vento had seen Pedro in Milwaukee. Vento was vague and would not confirm or deny Barnes' story saying simply that he did not remember.

Disgusted, they decided to return to Vegas. They had more questions now, especially about the mysterious Pedro. Before they arrived in Vegas late that night, Smith and Ridgway had a chance to talk privately on the plane about how sensitive Alioto had been since the solo interview by Smith. They agreed not to talk walking through the terminal when Alioto could not hear to avoid annoying him. Much had happened since they left Ocala only one week ago.

An interview with Ed Slade was arranged through his attorney for the following morning. They met at Slade's home where he was shown a photo lineup. He correctly picked Pedro out as the second man at the motel during the stolen antiques purchase. He agreed to look for the original Gary Johnson receipt. He knew it was underneath the kitchen sink where the plumbing entered the wall. On his hands and knees, sheepishly glancing over his shoulder at the investigators, Slade broke some dry wall and fished out the receipt.

"I didn't know that stuff was stolen at the time," he said, nervously brushing off his trousers. "I just thought it was a good deal from people who needed cash quick." He said his wife first told him in June 1987, that the things were stolen. "And I ask you," he added, "who could believe a crazy dame like her?"

Since Barnes had admitted Pedro was with him in Las Vegas and Slade had identified Pedro as being at the motel, the next move was to talk to Jim Baum and Jeff Bergman again. When shown his photo, however, both men insisted that they had never seen Pedro.

Ridgway was growing weary and was grateful for a schedule that demanded his presence in Ocala. After they took him to the airport, Alioto and Smith resumed their investigation. This time, they journeyed to nearby LaLuna Penitentiary outside El Paso to talk to Pedro.

The man brought to the interview room seemed as austere as the barren land around this federal detention center. Pedro glared coldly at Smith and Alioto as they advised him of his right to remain silent, which was his exact intention. He had an emaciated, drugged-out appearance with the disposition of a horned lizard.

Alioto explained that this interview was in reference to the Wayside Antiques robbery and murders in Florida. Pedro's vacant eyes were accentuated with dark circles as he delivered his only blunt comment in a distinct Mexican accent.

"*No comprehende.* You're wasting your time and mine." That was the end of the interview. The detectives headed back to Houston to see Lewis Barnes.

◆

21

The detectives revisited the Harris County Jail where a lackadaisical Lewis Barnes was confronted with his lies. Frank was seething as he spoke in low tones. "We have Felix's payroll records from Gilby. He was there, not with you. We have witnesses in Florida and Nevada who identified you and Pedro. Whatever you tell us we'll check out. Damn it, Lewis, that's what we have been doing for the last two weeks." Alioto pounded his fist on the table.

Lewis felt the rage of both men sitting close to him in the small room and it was unsettling. "I didn't shoot anybody, and that's the truth," he blurted anxiously. "I want to tell you all about it but I can't. I'll be killed if I tell you. They'll kill me and they'll kill my family." He began to cry.

Leo and Frank, immune to tears, each talked incessantly to convince Lewis that no one was going to hurt him. "Steps will be taken by all of us to protect your family," Leo assured him. "The Texas Rangers will help, even Sheriff Yeager in Missouri has promised protection. For God's sake, man, help yourself and tell us the truth."

Finally, at 5:30 p.m., September 30th, Lewis Wesley Barnes began a more accurate confession to the Wayside Antiques robbery and murders. He said that he and Pedro alone committed the robbery in his stolen 1976 blue Ford pickup with the white camper. They visited the store identifying items to steal and established the pattern of purchase, deposit, and late pickups. He clarified specifics such as bringing handcuffs and Pedro's using the store's pistol for the murders before disposing of it.

Lewis talked about Milwaukee as a frequent stopping place and that an antique auction there sold three-thousand dollars worth from the first robbery. He said that he and Pedro had stopped there on their way to Florida.

"When we get to Milwaukee this time, we looked, I mean Pete didn't have no drugs or anything and Shorty (Vento) tells him where to get the drugs in Chicago. Pete knows where he's talking about. There's Mexicans, like an all Mexican street. We go there and we do that and when Pete gets his drugs we head on to Florida."

"Did Shorty meet Pete?" asked Alioto.

"Yes."

"Did you do any crimes on the way to Florida?" Lewis shook his head no, staring at the floor.

"Tell us what happens when you get to Florida," led Alioto.

"I showed Pete the place first."

"What place are you talking about?" asked Leo, who had the tape running.

"The antique store, Wayside Inn. I show him that place. It was late, you know, it was already closed up and it wasn't dark yet. I took him to look at a gun shop down the road. We drove around a lot of places and looked. We didn't do anything but look." He glanced up for Leo's reaction, but seeing none, continued. "So we go back close to where the Wayside Antique store is and go up the road where there's a motel and we stay there."

"Was the motel on the Interstate?"

"Yes, sir," he said to Leo.

"Was it just the two of you checked into one room?"

"Yeah," Barnes replied.

"Alright," said Alioto, leaning forward. "You paid cash?" Lewis nodded. "Did you give a phoney name?"

"Always do," smiled Lewis.

"Do you remember the name you used?"

"Not right off hand."

"What happened next?"

"Well, we cased the place for two or three days. We'd go up there and park the truck in a field and watch. People kept coming to the house. So we left, and mosquitoes were real bad too, but we went again. We kept noticing a light on the back. It wasn't too much movement but the old man went to the store."

"So you kept coming back night after night," Alioto interrupted.

"Yeah, and about the second or third night, I told him there's people in here man. We can't do it. So we go to the gun shop and we found out the people lived in the back of the gun shop too. We go back again and there's only a light that stayed on in the trailer and nobody was doing anything. I told Pete I was nervous about it, afraid that people stayed in that trailer. I didn't know the first time. We go back to the motel and Pete's getting real mad and shouted are you going to do it or not? I said well, let's wait one more night. Pete tells me to call the people and tell them we're coming over and get the stuff we bought. I said I might as well. I'd paid him all but a few bucks and I could take it with me anyway. So we went back over to the place."

Lewis explained how he went in to pick up his layaway with Mr. Branum after they closed. Pete followed, a little behind. After the payment, Lewis told Branum that his mother sold antiques and that's why he knew the good ones.

"Were both the man and the woman in the store at this time?" asked Alioto.

"I couldn't see the woman because she was in the office. I remember she was talking on the phone to somebody when I first got there, but she hung up. The old man started talking about some paintings and Pete was right behind me. Then things got kinda crazy. I didn't, you know, we didn't have no guns on us or nothing."

"What happened first when you say things "got crazy." Explain that."

"Well, like I say, I was standing there and he was telling me how much the paintings were worth. I was standing by the door and Pete kinda come beside me and it was a rifle hanging. I think it was hanging there on the side of the wall. Pete grabbed it and run over by the lady and grabbed her by the arm. She had just got off the phone and he pulls her over to sit. He comes over close to me and the old man tried to grab the rifle and pull out the drawer to grab a gun. He was gonna hit him and the old man backed up and said, 'Don't hurt her, don't hurt me. We'll give you whatever you want.'"

"Everything happened so fast and I guess he was afraid of Pete hitting him with the rifle. The pistol was right there in plain sight. I was standing like a few feet from it. The man could have grabbed the gun that's what he was going for, but he didn't."

"What happened next?" asked Leo.

"Pete grabs the pistol, grabs it real quick and he jumps back beside me. It was a .22 revolver, an old western type. Everyone was out there just hollering, saying, 'Don't hurt us, we'll get you anything you want.' Pete asks how to open the safe and she looks to a file and says, 'I've got it all right here...how to open the safes.' She said *safes*. He said, 'What safes?' and she said, 'There's more in the back.' He makes her get up and she goes to a little file on her desk. She's real nervous. She's shaking. She's getting them out and spills it on the floor. She picks up a bunch of little cards with the safe numbers, the combinations of the safes, and he asks her where they're at. He lays the rifle down and has the pistol now. He wants me to tie them up. I was still real nervous and panicky, not doing anything and he says, 'Here,' and he reached in his back pocket and gave me handcuffs. I put the handcuffs on him and her and walked them out of the room and to the steps going upstairs. We set them on the bottom step and she's pointing to a little room right there and says, 'That's where you'll find all the safes.' She says, 'Just open it and get the stuff out of here,' because she's expecting some people.

"I handcuffed them at the stairway. Pete was holding the gun. I helped him open the one safe. It was cool. Everything opened right up with the combination. Then he couldn't get the old safe to open, the big one, so he asked the old man if he can open it. He said 'Yes, just don't hurt us.' We take him in the little room and there's only one chair there. We sat the woman down, she's real panicky, and I told her, 'Just be real calm, lady, nothing's going to happen to you.' She asked for a drink of water, I got it for her, and gave it to her in the mouth. She had her hands cuffed. The old man opens the safe for him. Pete put all the stuff in a black suitcase. Both safes just had rings in them. They're both hollering their heads off and we had to tape their mouths shut. I don't remember if I taped them or he taped them."

"Where did the tape come from?"

"Where they boxed the stuff up," Lewis answered.

"We just leave them there and go to picking everything up, putting it in boxes, and we take it to the back. The truck ain't there yet. Pete says to get the pickup and back it up while he gets more stuff. I go around front and get the pickup and pull it round back and while I'm loading I hear a shot. I run in the building real quick, inside to that little room."

"What did you see?" Leo asked quietly, remembering his own vision of the scene.

"I seen Pete standing there and he had a gun wrapped with a sweater and the sweater was smoking. The old man had blood running out of his head, like a real fast stream of blood shooting out of his head. The old woman was really trying to scream but she can't with the tape on her mouth. I like went crazy with Pete. I asked him what the fuck he was doing. I said to leave them alone. 'You're not supposed to do nothing like this.' He said, 'I'm not leaving anybody to testify against me. You get out of here. Go on.' As I was turning he shot again and I ran to the back door and I think I heard another shot.

"I got sick. I threw up on the ground. There wasn't hardly nothing else to load and he comes out and has the black suitcase. It was full of blood all over it and Pete had blood all over him. I was getting real sick. The truck was loaded and we left. His hands start shaking real bad. I'm hollering at him and he tells me to shut the fuck up. He's not going to leave no witnesses. Then he rolled down the window and he throws out the gun. We're over a viaduct. He asked me was that a road under there or a river. I told him I didn't know. He threw it out the window."

Alioto tried to pinpoint where the gun had been tossed, but Lewis only remembered that they never stopped the truck. It was night and they were crossing a railed highway bridge. When questioned about the sweater around the gun, Lewis said Pedro was wearing the sweater but it got caught in the safe door when he shut it. He yanked it loose, but a piece of it was left there.

Smith was encouraged with the description of the murder scene. Only a few technicians and himself had known about the sweater in the safe door. He had no doubt that Barnes was present in the room the night of the murders, although some details were still missing.

Follow-up questions established that Pedro and Lewis drove from Florida directly to San Antonio. Lewis delivered his drug buy and Pedro traded some clocks for personal drugs. After that, they went north to Dakota.

In North Dakota, according to Lewis, Pedro complained about Lewis to his brothers. "'He's not worth a shit. A no-good partner. The people were there and he didn't want to do it.'" Lewis sneered as he recounted Pedro's report.

"His brother Felix asked Pedro, 'Who did the killings?'

'I did them both,' answered Pedro. 'I shot them both.'

'Then you should get most of the money,' suggested Felix.

'I'll get mine,' Pedro answered with a menacing glare. 'I want somebody to buy it that can give me my money at one time.'"

Lewis concluded the interview with an account of how he got rid of the merchandise. "There was about seven-hundred dollars in the safe and I had some drug money left, but we were running low. Pulling antiques around in my truck wasn't safe. I went and got the rest of my money from Shorty. We picked up drugs for Pete in Chicago and then went to Las Vegas. We drove all the way. I live there already and I have a little storage place there. When we get there I talked to James."

"Diamond Jim?"

"Yeah, Diamond Jim. He says the guy that buys stuff was gone, to be back in a day or two. I go unload and Pete finds out where my little storage room was. I had a couple of little mink coats there too that was Terry's."

"And then you sell the antiques while you and Pete are in Vegas?" Smith tried to keep him on track.

"Diamond Jim gets to the old man that buys them and I talk to him while Pete waits in the car at the bottom of the hill. I'd already met him several times because I sold him some silver and other stuff. He says he'd like the antiques but will only give me so much on the dollar. He said to put them in a motel and he'd come over that night. He gave me this number to call, and said he'd give me a price when he saw them. It was about seven or eight o'clock. It was right at dark. He comes over, looks at them, and likes what he sees."

"Was Pete there when he came in?"

"Yeah, he was in the motel room and we had them

strung out there except the two gold chairs were in the truck."

"So the old man sees Pete in the motel room?"

"Yeah, and he gave us seventeen-five. I'd already told Pete they'd bring about twenty-five-thousand easy, but he thought the man's price was alright. I told the man right there that people had been killed over this stuff and he says, 'I don't care. I'm going to put the stuff away in the dungeons I have and there ain't nobody ever gonna find it.'"

"What did you and Pete do after the deal was over?" Alioto wanted to wind things up.

"When the old man give me the money right there at the motel I handed it to Pete. Then I take Pete back to San Antonio."

The final details were wrapped up by Frank and Leo. The men wore gloves that they found in the store. The shots were very close together, seconds, not minutes apart. The victims were cooperative and gave them no reason to murder them. The entire interview was recorded on tape.

Finally, the only promise made to Lewis was that the detectives would stand by him and make it known that he told the truth. Lewis, who was in no position to bargain, had to be content with that — for now.

◆

22

Smith and Alioto's offices at MCSO would have been physically too close even if the desks had been in different counties. Therefore, they distanced themselves from each other on their return by going in opposite directions during their investigation.

Leo looked for the murder weapon that had been tossed over a viaduct, even though the search after three-and-a-half years was probably hopeless. Volunteers with machetes and metal detectors checked every overpass north of Wayside on I-75. Records of guns found since July 1984 in Marion and Alachua Counties were also checked. The .22 Ruger, which Leo looked for, did not turn up.

Alioto picked up investigator Ed Phillips and went out to Irvine to show Marty Gates his photo display of suspects. Gates, who had identified Barnes previously, now positively identified Pedro Covarrubias as one of the two customers at Wayside just prior to the robbery. Pedro's photo remarkably resembled the original artist's sketch.

The following week, Ric Ridgway announced that the State Attorney's Office would ask the Grand Jury to indict a suspect in the murders. The man, being held in a Houston jail, was described as a thirty-two-year-old native of Missouri. His name was withheld since he had not yet been charged. Newspapers reported the pending charges in Texas plus the details of the murders and subsequent nationwide investigation. David Branum, Jr. followed this with great anticipation.

"In recent weeks," an article stated, "investigators spent more than $100,000 and traveled to more than a dozen states..." The public was beginning to realize the scope of this case.

At a press conference, Alioto and Smith described how they first traced the man by aliases, determined his real name through interviews and traced him to Texas through an examination of telephone records.

The Grand Jury was scheduled to be impaneled on October 22, 1987. Initially, Ridgway invited only Leo Smith to testify with the explanation that Smith had been on the case since day one.

"Why use two people when you can do it with just one?" Ridgway surmised. Besides, there would be no chance of conflicting testimony if only one version was told.

Alioto was livid. As head of the Task Force he felt

that he should appear before the Grand Jury. Being a hard man to shake was the very quality that made him an excellent cop. After a few phone calls, he was added to the list to testify. His case telephone analysis, timelines, and aliases chart became the centerpiece of the presentation.

On October 23rd, Lewis Wesley Barnes, a.k.a. Gary Barnes, Gary Johnson, and Jerry Johnson, was indicted on two counts of first degree murder by the Marion County Grand Jury. He was also indicted on a charge of armed robbery.

Reporters hustled for information.

Sgt. Ken Engle, MCSO spokesman, told them, "Barnes will be arrested on the Marion County charges as soon as possible. He is scheduled to go on trial in Houston, Texas on November 3rd, for attempted murder of two public safety narcotics officers."

"When is he going to be brought here?" they asked.

"Depending on what happens in Houston. We don't know when he will be arrested on these charges."

"What about the second suspect?" a reporter pressed.

"Due to the complexity of the case, we're not commenting on anything other than Lewis Barnes," replied Engle firmly.

When questions were directed at Al Lee, a spokesman for the State Attorney's Office, he said, "Extradition proceedings will begin immediately. If he doesn't fight the extradition, he could be here by the end of November. If Barnes does fight extradition, it could take until mid-January to bring him to Florida."

The other suspect was identified only as being in federal prison on drug charges, not eligible for parole until 1991, some four years. Obviously, there was time to present a case against him also.

On November 20th, Barnes pled guilty in Texas and was sentenced to forty years in prison with a mandatory minimum of ten years. Dan Rizzo, who prosecuted Barnes in Harris County, Texas, said, "I can't be sure who will get the next opportunity to prosecute Barnes. I know of a hold from somewhere out west and I also know he's got a warrant pending from somewhere near San Antonio. I don't know who's going to get first dibs on him."

On December 18th, Barnes waived extradition to Marion County. Assistant State Attorney Jim Phillips announced that his office was filing the necessary paperwork with state officials in Tallahassee. "Barnes should be returned here sometime in early January," he said.

Alioto and Smith were convinced that Barnes was eager to return to Florida. Smith sagely summed it up for the reporters. "Barnes is afraid he'll be killed in Texas prison for implicating a possible accomplice in the Wayside killings."

Before Barnes' trial began, it was imperative to get the recovered robbery evidence to Florida. Smith and Alioto flew to Las Vegas and spent four days insuring that the antiques and art objects were packed securely. They personally drove them back to Ocala in a rented van. The long-awaited day came on January 12, 1988 in Houston, when Lewis Wesley Barnes was transferred into the custody of Alioto and Smith. During the flight, Barnes repeatedly reminded the detectives of their promise to protect his family. He requested that he be allowed to marry the mother of his children. He also asked that Terry and their children be relocated to Missouri near his family.

By eleven o'clock that same night, Barnes was booked into the Marion County Jail on the Grand Jury charges. Word had spread throughout the compound about the arrival of the "big time" operator.

Barnes' first court appearance was held the next morning when Assistant Public Defender Charles Holloman was appointed his attorney.

◆

23

The Wayside Antique murders were the most notorious and intriguing unsolved crimes ever known in Marion County. Since the antique recovery in Vegas, the case had become the media's constant focal point. The public was engrossed in it. Even inmates at the Marion County Jail knew enough about this slick criminal to make him a jailhouse celebrity. Most of them were aware of the numerous warrants nationwide for his arrest. He had reputedly transported drugs through many states without getting caught. He was known as a master thief and accomplished escape artist whom jails could not hold. They knew he masked his identity using false names and disguises. This was the stuff that made folk heroes.

Corrections officers viewed Barnes as the ultimate challenge. They used special procedures in the C-pod maximum security cell block for such a high risk prisoner.

He was given bright orange overalls that identified him as a capital offender, then locked in a one-man cell. The cell was an area of eighty-three square feet and contained a single bed, a small table, and a toilet. There was one tall window only five inches wide and an adjacent ventilator window just ten inches wide. He was allowed out of his cell for forty-five minutes each day to exercise under close supervision, and when he was in the cell he was checked every fifteen minutes.

The new prison was the pride of the area and it was considered perhaps the finest in the state. Barnes, of course, was not overjoyed about the accommodations, but he seemed to like being recognized by other inmates. After one week he bragged to them, "I won't be here long. No more than a couple of months." Based on what they had heard, they believed him. Many offered to help if he would take them along. Here was a man who lived by his wits and had the skills, it seemed, to back up his boasts.

Leo Smith felt relieved that his work in this case was finished except for testifying at the trial, which was scheduled to begin March 15th. Not so with Frank Alioto. He was busy building a case against Pedro Covarrubias.

The walk down the echoing hall into the sterile interview room to talk to Lewis Barnes became a ritual for Frank. They were on a first name basis now, a routine had been established. In return for each new piece of verifiable information about Pedro, Lewis would ask a favor of Frank.

The detective made extensive notes and checked out everything. He was told about an incident involving Pedro in Corpus Christi where he sold watches from the robbery.

"He bragged about the murders to this guy," Lewis said, "and told him the watches were from that robbery. I'm sure Pete had dealt with him before but talk like that makes me nervous."

"What was the man's name?"

"Chris Cortez was the name he used. I don't know, but I can tell you where to find him."

Alioto and Ridgway were soon talking to a petrified Chris Cortez. He admitted knowing Pedro and Lewis, but that's all. He feared the Mexican Mafia more than the authorities and he knew that Pedro was connected.

Later at the jail, Lewis agreed to let FDLE give him a polygraph test. In their opinion, Barnes was telling the truth by saying that he did not shoot the Branums and that Pedro had pulled the trigger.

He detailed how Pedro would not let him out of his sight until he had cash from the robbery. They were together in Milwaukee, where the antiques were stored for a short time, and he recalled that jewelry was sold to Steve Vento and his relatives.

This information looked promising since Frank and Ridgway remembered some of the heist was wrapped in newspapers from that city. They were disappointed to find that the storage rental building mentioned no longer existed. When the company was finally located, they were able to produce the actual rental receipt and the detective took a copy of it for evidence.

They decided to talk to Steve Vento again, who already knew that Barnes had been convicted in Texas and was waiting for trial in Ocala. This time he talked more freely with animated gestures as he explained his association with Pedro.

"Yes, I saw Pete here. All I remember is that he was Spanish and had blotch marks on his face. He was extremely involved in narcotics. He was a weird kind of character who made me feel uncomfortable. I just wanted to get away from him."

Regardless of the questions, somehow Vento's answers always included references to his acting or casino careers. Obviously, he enjoyed talking about himself more than others, but he did acknowledge helping arrange storage for Lewis. However, he strongly denied making any purchases from either man.

When Alioto returned to Ocala, he started making arrangements for the jailhouse wedding that Barnes wanted. It was an accepted policy to allow marriages to take place in jail when late-term pregnancies or children were involved, so he contacted Sheriff Moreland for clearance. Both the Sheriff and Ridgway reviewed and approved Frank's request.

Two days before Valentine's Day, a smiling Lewis Barnes joined Terry in a prison administrative office where Alioto had arranged for the wedding to take place. Alioto's secretary, a Florida Notary Public, stood solemnly before the couple to perform the ceremony. Only their youngest child was present. Even in this austere situation, Terry was radiantly happy to be officially married. When Alioto offered a small cake that he had purchased for the occasion, her large brown eyes could no longer contain the tears.

The simple ceremony was kept very quiet for reasons of security. A note was put on the marriage license saying: "Please do not publish." It was signed by Sheriff Moreland. After the brief wedding ceremony, Terry was sent back home with no conjugal visit allowed. As if bells had rung, word of the marriage spread throughout the jailhouse population. They concluded that Barnes was indeed special.

The marriage had been Barnes' first priority. With that accomplished, he conjured up other schemes to stir things up for his benefit. He decided to call FBI Special Agent Michael Cervellera to come in for a talk. When he arrived, Barnes complained about the actions of the MCSO after his arrest in Texas in September 1987. In return for hearing those and other complaints, he tossed the agent scraps of information. He said that on the day of the murders he had picked up a shipment of cocaine in South Florida.

"I still have thirty chicken boxes full of sixteen kilos each," he smiled as the interview ended.

Cervellera had to assess what he had heard, but his interest had been peaked. He found a confidential source within the prison who knew a lot about Barnes. He listened passively while the informant told about Barnes being a mule for a large-scale drug importer in Houston, Texas. This was well documented although the names he gave would prove helpful. When he began talking about a possible jail break, the agent snapped to attention.

"Tell me what you know about this," he demanded.

"Barnes said he had the whole escape planned out," he paused, leaning forward as he lowered his voice. "He plans to climb into the *plumbing chase*. The maintenance men leave it open and he could crawl through right up to the roof."

Cervellera immediately checked this out with Capt. John Pauls, head of the jail. The plumbing chase was indeed left open and could have been used for an escape. In less than a month as their guest, Barnes knew things about the jail that his keepers did not know.

On March 1, 1988, Special Agent Matthew Hall, FBI, Houston, responded to Cervellera's inquiry about Barnes. He confirmed that druglord Roque Garcia was criminally active and, until his arrest in September 1987, Barnes was his right-hand man.

"Barnes' Texas criminal history is unbelievable," reported Hall. "Sixteen aliases, several birthdates, and at least four social security numbers."

"I'm familiar with some of that," replied Cervellera in a patronizing manner, but he had to laugh aloud at Hall's final remark.

"Barnes should be considered an escape risk," he warned.

Cervellera already knew that, too.

◆

24

When Barnes learned that he could make long-distance calls from the inmate telephone in Pod A, he was literally back in business. He had six ounces of heroin to begin with and he searched among the prisoners for someone to help him prime the pump with it. He found a likely candidate, unaware that he was also the snitch who helped the FBI.

"It's stuff I own," Barnes told him confidentially one day, "and I have it stashed."

"Six ounces, huh? That's good," said the snitch. "I'll see what I can do. I have some marijuana connections locally."

"Fine. I can put any kind of drug deal together," smiled Barnes, his mind racing. "I can put a heroin deal together through a guy in Milwaukee. He's hunting for pot and moves by the pound. I can arrange for Martens to exchange heroin for the marijuana. It'll work."

"Sounds like a sweet deal to me," agreed the snitch. "I'll get in touch with my source and we'll work it out."

Instead, he contacted Agent Cervellera, who in turn coordinated with FDLE, MCSO, and Ocala Police to establish an undercover agent as a buyer. They told the informant to negotiate with Barnes and they would set up the bust.

Barnes was in his element now. He cheerfully made phone calls to work out the details. His proposal was inspired. He would let the six ounces of heroin go for seven-thousand dollars worth of marijuana. Cash would be paid up to fifty pounds of additional homegrown merchandise.

One week later, on March 8, 1988, Cervellera had MCSO request permission to monitor Barnes' telephone conversations. Ridgway's legal advice was that no permission was needed because signs posted over phones in the Marion County Jail clearly stated:

> NOTICE: FOR SECURITY PURPOSES ALL TELEPHONES IN THIS JAIL ARE SUBJECT TO BEING MONITORED.

Therefore, he said, "There is no expectation of privacy," and the conversations could be monitored or recorded. FDLE legal counsel, Craig Rockstein, was also consulted and concurred. A monitor was promptly set up and soon they had the data on the deal.

The drug exchange was set up for Tuesday morning, March 14th at the Davis Brothers' Motor Lodge on West 40 in Ocala. Steve Martens brought the 6.7 ounces of heroin from Milwaukee and met the undercover agent, who had the marijuana with him. During the transaction, a law enforcement team roared up to the motel, made the arrests, and seized the drugs. There was a suitcase full of cash in Marten's Oldsmobile, which was parked outside, and the cash and car were also confiscated.

MCSO officer Sgt. Patty Lumpkin, who had been an integral part of the arrest, spoke to the media. "We've never seized that much heroin in Marion County before. It must be worth a quarter-of-a-million dollars."

Alioto sent an urgent memo to the jail asking that Barnes not be charged at this time. He said that it would serve no purpose considering Barnes' circumstances and may inhibit productive talks with him.

Authorities, pressed by public demand, insisted on full charges. Martens was charged with trafficking in heroin, possession with intent to deliver, conspiracy to traffic, and possession of marijuana. Barnes, although locked in jail and in spite of Alioto's request, was charged with trafficking in heroin and conspiracy to traffic. A bond of more than one-and-a-half million was placed on each man, a technicality in Barnes' case.

The public was shocked. How could Lewis Barnes organize and implement the huge drug deal while being imprisoned in a maximum security jail?

Barnes languidly accepted his growing reputation among the inmates and corrections personnel. The arrest confirmed his boasts of assets and widespread connections, and he never showed concern about the quarter-million dollar loss. He played it cool for his growing audience.

"I have stuff stashed in several other states," he boasted, "and it's just no problem getting either drugs or cash."

Even the guards were tempted as he approached a chosen few. He offered them ten times their year's salary just to turn their heads the other way. He quietly propositioned them, offering half the cash up front and the other half when he was free. As these rumors spread, the jail became alive with interest, but news of it was contained within the prison walls. *Money talks and prisoner walks*, gleefully thought Barnes.

Since his trial had been delayed due to the new charges, Barnes continued working with Alioto as usual.

"Maybe my wife can tell you more about Pete," he suggested. "He traveled with us from Milwaukee to Las Vegas selling the antiques. She said he tried to hit on her saying I'd lost my courage at Wayside and that he was the main character in the job."

"She was afraid of Pete?" asked Alioto.

"We were both afraid of him because of what he'd done. He was hanging on for his share, but we wanted to split. When we sold the stuff and Pete got his money, we couldn't get away from him fast enough."

Alioto did talk to Terry and she said basically the same as Barnes. Pedro had talked to her about the robbery and murders on the trip. He took full credit for the job, but according to her, never said that he actually killed two people.

There was an unexpected surprise in April. Ridgway, who had been on the Barnes case from the beginning and had met all of the potential witnesses, abruptly resigned as Assistant State Attorney. Politics was the reason. He was a campaign organizer for Democrat Brad King's bid to unseat Ridgway's boss, State Attorney Ray Gill. Resigning from the Barnes prosecution left him free to openly criticize Gill, and he was hired as a legal advisor to Sheriff Don Moreland. Since there had been added charges, changes in defense attorney, and it was not clear who the prosecutor would be, a status conference on the trial was scheduled before Judge Victor Musleh on Monday, April 25th.

Barnes seemed unaffected by all this and continued to test the corrections officers. In defiance of the rules, he hung his towel over the ten-inch ventilator to dry. He would remove it when told to do so, but he always put it back. During the next three weeks, the towel hung there most of the time. The guards gradually accepted it as a nuisance not worth the trouble of changing.

On Friday, April 23, 1988, Marion County Jail got a new resident, Bernard Ellis, Jr. He had been brought over from the Florida Mental Hospital in Chattahoochee and placed in the cell directly above Lewis Barnes. Ellis had been arrested the preceding August for lewd and lascivious conduct in the presence of a child. Now the hospital had declared him mentally competent to stand trial. He was destined to figure prominently in Lewis Barnes' life.

◆

25

On Saturday morning, the day after his arrival, Bernard Ellis was released for his forty-five-minute exercise time. His wild eyes darted all around as he left his cell and walked to the outside railing which surrounded the second tier. To the amusement of the guard, his movements were quick and elf-like. He grasped the railing and leaned over it, laughing. Suddenly, his feet shot straight up in the air and he was suspended upside down. Frozen in slow motion, the astonished guard watched as Ellis plummeted to the cement below. His skull hit with a sickening thud, directly in front of Barnes' cell, splattering blood everywhere. Some of the prisoners who saw the incident sent up a deafening roar that gained continuing momentum. Joining the din, some screamed, some sang hymns, while others beat on their doors. Soon there was bedlam. The inmates began shouting accusations and threats at the officers for delaying medical treatment. They yelled, "Killers, pigs, butchers!"

After a seemingly long time, medical assistance arrived and Ellis was removed and taken to Munroe Regional Medical Center. This did not end the disturbance. The clamor lasted long after Ellis had been removed and the bloody mess had been cleaned.

By morning things were back to near normal routine and breakfast was served at six o'clock as usual. As the tray was pushed through the opening at Barnes' cell 107, an inmate shouted.

"You can save that tray for me," he jeered. "That one took a long walk."

The trustee stared through the door window at the still figure lying under bed sheets. His eyes moved to the broken window. The adjoining ventilator had been torn out of the wall and was hanging loose in the opening.

"My, God!" he said aloud and ran to call the sergeant on duty. They entered the cell and could not believe the incredible escape scene.

Barnes had stuffed his orange prison jumpsuit with paper bags and had put it in the bed as a decoy. He then removed an angle-iron crossbrace from the bed and used it as a pry bar. He broke the plexiglass window and reached outside to pry the ventilator away from the cement wall. Slowly he bent back the quarter-inch steel ventilator frame until he could squeeze his way through. He was cut forcing his way through the jagged opening and left a trail of blood across the grass to the twelve-foot chainlink perimeter fence. Barnes had wrapped himself in a wool blanket to cross the one-hundred foot grassy yard. Since the fence was topped with barbed wire, he decided to go through it. He used a tool to unthread an opening in the fence and wiggled through. He left the blanket, tool, and a small piece of bed sheet behind. Once outside the fence he could see Interstate 75, which ran behind the prison. Soon a trucker stopped and picked him up and Barnes was on his way.

At 6:50 Sunday morning, April 23rd, Barnes became the first escapee from the two-year-old, 8.7 million dollar jail. The FBI was notified and issued an escape warrant. When authorities in Missouri and Texas were contacted, it was determined that Barnes' wife was also missing. Barnes had a huge head start and could now be anywhere.

The internal investigation of the escape showed no mercy. Inmates were made to reveal that Lewis had been working on the opening for at least four days. The towel had hidden his tenacious efforts at prying the ventilator loose. Obviously, the fifteen-minute eye checks were not made, just logged. The last time Barnes was positively known to be in his cell was midnight during the chaotic disturbance over the Ellis accident. This meant that Barnes could have been gone for almost seven hours before he was discovered missing.

In addition to a well-executed escape, Barnes had laid the groundwork to cover his tracks. He had told different stories to various inmates about where he would go.

Included were destinations to Mexico, Missouri, and several other states.

Ironically, he took time to leave a letter under his mattress for Alioto. In it he blamed the detective for his escape. Lewis claimed that Frank had not done enough for him. He declared that he had not killed anyone and should not be charged with murder. He considered escape his only option.

Don Moreland had never had such an embarrassment as this in his sixteen years as sheriff. Not only had Barnes escaped Marion County's state-of-the-art jail, but he was acknowledged to be the most dangerous and desperate prisoner detained there. In the intense media coverage, Moreland was direct and offered no excuses.

"It simply boiled down to human error of eight people," Moreland told reporters. "When you operate a jail you cannot be lax for one second."

Maj. J.P. Holland, jail director, and Capt. John Pauls, jail administrator, agonized over answers to questions such as why no one saw or heard Barnes working on the escape window. Within five days three corrections officers responsible for checking Barnes were fired. Five sergeants were demoted including the on-duty sergeant, who was permanently reduced to the lowest rank and lost one-third of his salary. These were the most severe dismissals and demotions in a single case on record.

Moreland's anger and humiliation knew no bounds. He vowed to get Barnes back in jail and tried for the Wayside murders. The day after the escape he called

Alioto in and told him succinctly to find him. Immediately, Frank was on a flight to San Antonio in hot pursuit.

◆

26

Barnes squatted on the free side of the prison fence very pleased with himself, and reached back through the opening for his sandals. He froze and listened carefully. As far as he could tell, there was no new activity about the jail. He used the blanket to clean himself, and decided that the white tee shirt covered enough of his boxer undershorts to pass for any other casually dressed Floridian. He started a fast walk through the heavy brush toward the lights and sounds of Interstate 75.

When he reached the highway, he walked in the northbound lane until he found a few trucks parked on the side of the road. A driver was awake in one of the trucks and Lewis tapped on his door to ask for a ride. The driver seemed happy to have someone to talk to, and the story Lewis told him was loosely the truth.

"I, ah, just got out of a bad situation and I'm going to

see my wife and family in Texas," he explained as they hit the highway. Lewis was full of stories about previous trips on I-75 and praised the Gainesville rest areas. After a while they stopped at one and he hurriedly placed a collect call to his mother in Missouri and his wife in San Antonio. Both women were delighted that he was on the road again.

Lewis rode with the rig until they came to the Interstate 10 crossing. Since the driver was continuing north on I-75, Lewis jumped out with a smile and a wave at the rest stop there. He didn't wait long. Soon a weary driver pulled up in his pickup truck, slammed the door, and ran urgently to the men's room.

"Yes," whistled Lewis through the gap in his teeth, and was happily back on the highway before the owner had flushed the toilet. Looking around in the cab, Lewis laughed out loud at his luck. There were two cartons of cigarettes on the seat and a change of clothes on a hanger. Keeping rhythm to a lively tune on the radio, he continued west. He would be out of Florida just after daybreak and he knew Houston was less than twelve hours of hard driving away.

About four in the morning, he spotted a busy gas station, pulled up to an outside pump and called in for a fill up. When he finished pumping, he watched until the one clerk was busy and left without paying. Once he was out of Florida, he pulled into a stop and sold the two cartons of cigarettes at discount prices. He rewarded himself with a good meal and called his former employers in Houston. His contact agreed to have a car and cash waiting for him upon arrival in Houston late Sunday.

When the gas Lewis bought with the rest of the cigarette money was running low, he pulled into a rest area in Louisiana. He was on the short connector of Interstate 12, which connects the two ends of Interstate 10 where it dips south of Lake Pontchartrain to New Orleans. He was out of Florida, through the short runs of Alabama and Mississippi and on the last leg to Texas. Rather than risk stealing gas in mid-afternoon, he decided to dump the truck and hitch a ride on to Houston.

He parked the little pickup in the car area and walked casually over to where the big rigs were parked. Within moments he found a ride to Houston where friends and a car waited. He was relieved on the ride not to hear any mention of an escaped murderer from Ocala, Florida.

The trucker told Lewis about a recent series of truck highjackings in the Houston area. Ironically, he was talking to one of the most successful of the bandits who was returning to his base of operation. Lewis listened with interest to the new safety procedures truckers were now using to avoid losing their loads and rigs. Lewis would have big news for his Houston accomplices.

Lewis hopped out at the predesignated location where a man met him in a new blue Oldsmobile. He went directly to a reserved room in a Houston hotel where clothes and cash awaited him. After he had a hot shower and meal, Lewis went to bed for the first time in several days.

He awoke Monday to a set schedule for the coming

week. Oral surgery had been arranged to fill the gap between his front teeth along with some other minor cosmetics to change his appearance. There would be a cooling-off period at the farm in southwest Texas, which Lewis knew to be a party place. He was ecstatic. After the four-thousand dollar tooth repair, he drove his new car across Texas to the farm. He spoke with his wife twice by phone, encouraged her to keep in touch, and said he would be back in San Antonio soon.

Lewis had been at the farm for short periods of time throughout his years in the crime organization. He had hidden money and drugs there for just such an emergency and he made careful plans on how to remain free. He had been a fugitive from the law most of his adult life, and he was surrounded by people in the same position. All supported each other, but he knew he had to be especially careful due to the serious charges, the frenzied police search since his escape, and the probable reward being offered for his capture.

◆

27

San Antonio is a city of scenic canals lined with taste-challenging Tex-Mex eateries where warm hospitality is prevalent, but Frank arrived there with tunnel vision. He headed directly to the FBI office to begin brainstorming sessions concerning Lewis Barnes' escape from Marion County Jail and how to find him. Agents and Texas Rangers agreed that his wife and children were the key: he would return for them given time. This sounded right to Frank. In fact, he had a five-thousand dollar check from the department made out to himself and Terry Barnes with hopes that the wife would trade the money for information. A Ranger volunteered to take him to Mother Julia's place so Frank could present the proposition to Terry.

"We're going to be looking for Lewis the rest of his life." Frank had Terry's undivided attention. "You can run with him or you can help us get him back. We will never stop looking until we catch him. We know his friends and where they operate. It's just a matter of time."

Terry nodded her head, wide-eyed. "The kids and I are tired of running," she explained rapidly, looking at each man in hopes they would understand. "I'm a young woman," she added, adjusting her full blouse and crossing her long legs. "I've got to get on with my life." The Ranger eyed her admiringly and thought she shouldn't have any problem doing that.

"I have something here that might help you make a decision," said Alioto, sticking to business. "If you help us catch Lewis, I have five-thousand dollars for you to help raise the children."

She smiled and looked him squarely in the eyes. "For that kind of money I'll help you any way I can." The Ranger wanted to talk about that, but Frank pressed on.

"You've heard from him?"

"Yes, I have. He said he'll come for us, but he didn't say when."

Both Terry and Julia agreed to help. Soon a phone trace was installed. One officer waited inside with a sawed-off shotgun while another sat in an unmarked car across the street. Rangers covered the day shift surveillance. Alioto and a federal agent took the night shift.

The first stakeout stint lasted an entire month for Alioto. Each night he sat at a front window as life in the busy house swirled about him. Since Felix, Julia's common-law husband, was in jail and Lewis had been absent as well, money was scarce. Everybody worked somewhere. Terry and her sister worked in a local bar and often brought men home with them. They would walk past Alioto, laughing in the dark and continue upstairs. Unnamed migrants constantly came and went. On many occasions the small three-bedroom house was packed.

Felix had been a migrant labor crew leader and his house was an information center and haven for transients. There was a continuous turnover of people. They knew why Frank was there and either ignored or tolerated him. They had heard about his help with the marriage and, more recently, with expenses.

For the first long month of surveillance, Lewis did not show up, but on Mother's Day he called Terry. Alert officers listened as he talked and cried, saying how much he missed her and the children. The long distance call was from a pay phone. It sounded like he would be coming back soon.

In an update to Sheriff Moreland, Frank told him they needed more publicity and public support. *America's Most Wanted* was a new television show in 1988 and Frank recommended using it to help capture Barnes. He was convinced the show was a good new police tool with broad reach.

Frank briefly returned to Ocala and was given the go ahead for televising the Barnes story. Producers were interested and the episode was immediately included in their schedule. Frank worked closely with them making it as accurate and authentic as possible. Actors resembling the wanted man and known principals were found and cast.

This accomplished, Frank returned to San Antonio to again become part of the stakeout. One day Julia appeared driving a recent model used car. The officers noted the license number and traced it. When they visited the city lot where the car had been purchased, the dealer said a young man came in his office with eight-thousand dollars cash in a brown paper bag. His instructions were to register the car to Julia and deliver it to her house. The dealer never knew Barnes' name but could identify him as the buyer from a photograph.

This was a solid indication that Barnes was at last in the area. A few days later, Rangers thought they saw Barnes ride by the house on a motorcycle. He was gone before they could pursue him. His children were playing in the front yard with some other neighborhood children but suspected nothing. Clearly, the hunted was stalking the bait, but the stakeout continued.

One night in the darkened living room as Frank stared out the front window, Julia pulled up a wooden chair and started talking about a conversation she had overheard between Pedro and Lewis. After their return to North Dakota from the robbery and murders, Pedro felt that he had done all the work and deserved the biggest share of the money.

"Did Pedro specifically mention killing the people?" Frank asked.

"He bragged a lot about the job," continued Julia, "and said Lewis did very little."

As Frank passed her an ashtray he silently hoped she would be willing to testify to that later. She inhaled one last time before extinguishing her cigarette. He hated the smoke, the uncomfortable chair, and the whole gig. He longed to get back to Ocala and begin work with the film crew.

◆

28

The television crew caused quite a stir in the small town of Ocala when they arrived August 11th. The show's producer, Michael Cerny, called the planned Barnes segment, "A 1980's Wanted Poster." He was happy to report that in its short run the show had helped capture twenty-five percent of the criminals featured.

Alioto was enthusiastic. "We couldn't buy this kind of publicity," he exclaimed. "When the show airs on September 18th, we expect someone to call in and say they've seen Barnes."

A casting search brought in Dallas actor Price Carson for the fugitive role. He had a gap between his front teeth and looked somewhat like Barnes. Carson was similar in build, was about the same age, and did a credible job of portraying Barnes. Periodically, actual footage of Barnes was used in the segment.

The Wayside murders were recreated with accuracy. This sequence was filmed in the shop where actors were handcuffed to the actual safes with their mouths taped. Sale of the stolen antiques from the Las Vegas motel was staged in a similar motel in Ocala, the Southland Motel on East Silver Springs Boulevard. The producers were given every possible detail about the case to make the film realistic. The escape sequence was filmed at the Marion County Jail where an actual window ventilator unit was used as well as the real fence.

Film crews went to Houston to shoot the initial chase and capture scenes on location there. The chase and gunfire with the Texas Rangers was excitingly realistic and enabled viewers to form an accurate picture of events and of the fugitive himself.

When the project was complete, Alioto returned to the San Antonio stakeout, confident that the production would provide the break needed to find Barnes.

The Fox Productions program was aired on September 18, 1988, and was a quality presentation. Fox had twenty-five hotline operators on duty from eight until midnight, who were capable of handling up to three thousand calls from viewers. Three-hundred-twenty-seven people called in after the show with leads on Barnes' whereabouts.

Significantly, two days after the show aired, a San Antonio resident called the FBI office. "I think I know that guy you're looking for on *America's Most Wanted*," he said. "I think I sold him a car." The man described the car as being a blue Oldsmobile and gave the tag number.

A second call gave the FBI a San Antonio address where the fugitive could be found. Agents hurried to the upper middle-class neighborhood on the opposite side of town from where the stake out had been held. They found a blue Oldsmobile in the driveway with the reported tag number. Responding as if he expected the visit, Lewis Barnes burst out of the house and drove away at high speed. The air became alive with radio communications as the agents took off after him. A multiple-unit chase was coordinated including helicopters, San Antonio Police, Sheriff's deputies from two counties, FBI agents, and Texas Rangers, all in hot pursuit. The agents were first to reach him at a large intersection but as they closed in, Barnes rammed their car, made a U-turn, and sped away. Soon he ran into a roadblock and damaged his own car. In a frenzied flight, he fled on foot to a residential neighborhood, chose a van to hot wire, and was off again.

The chase continued until Barnes came upon another roadblock of FBI cars across the highway. He desperately veered off the road and entered a cultivated field at high speed. The van became stuck in a field ditch and he fled once again on foot into the woods. A police bloodhound located Barnes buried under a pile of muddy logs. He was covered with large ants when he finally surrendered. He was carrying over ten-thousand dollars and a .25 caliber semiautomatic handgun.

Television news teams were close behind filming the chase and capture for local networks. The Sunday, September 25th capture was viewed in Ocala on Monday night. Local residents, including the victims' son, were now elated with Barnes' recapture.

The Texas Department of Corrections responded firmly. They sent a teletype demanding that Barnes not be released again to Florida authorities. Alioto issued this succinct response, "Texas wanted to keep him. Florida lost him. He was slippery." But it did not end there. Eventually the decision was made to allow Barnes to be released to Alioto.

Flying Barnes back to Orlando required incredible coordination. The airline was notified that one passenger was a dangerous fugitive and that investigators accompanying him would be armed. Barnes and his captors were to board the plane first. They were seated in the last row. Barnes wore leg irons and handcuffs, and neither he nor the officers were to leave their seats. Passengers were not made aware of the situation. When the plane landed, the three men were the last to disembark. Three cars and seven law enforcement officers escorted Barnes from Orlando to Marion County Jail.

Barnes arrived at 1:30 a.m. on Wednesday and was taken to the jail booking office. Six hours later as an extra precaution, Judge Hale Stancil came to the jail for Barnes' first court appearance. Although he had ten-thousand dollars when caught, he swore indigency and a public defender was appointed.

Every possible precaution was made to control Barnes. In a special memo to his staff, Jail Administrator Capt. John Pauls warned, "Do not be lulled into a false sense of security with this person. He is polite and does not seem to be the type of person you could not trust. He is considered to be *extremely dangerous*. Barnes will be moved to a new cell every day. He will be strip searched every day. He will not be permitted contact with other inmates. He will not be allowed outside the cell block without wrist and ankle chains."

The State Attorney estimated that a realistic trial date was the spring of 1989. There were doubts about who the prosecutor would be. Ric Ridgway was currently active in a political campaign to unseat his former boss, State Attorney Ray Gill. Gill favored Jim Phillips to handle the case. This would be resolved later.

◆

29

Barnes and Alioto talked openly with a mutual respect after the recapture, a situation similar to critique by opponents after a hard-fought sports contest. Barnes' candor was so disarming that Alioto warned others, "We have to be very careful not to underestimate him."

Frank wanted to tie up some loose ends. He was aware of speculation surrounding the escape and asked Barnes if he had outside help. Lewis told him that a trustee in the jail had stolen a small tool from a maintenance cart in exchange for some candy, but that he had acted alone.

"Remember my Dad's salvage yard in Missouri. I worked there. I can take anything apart," he reminded him. "With the tool from the trustee and the angle iron pry bar from the bed, in two or three days I dismantled the window and ventilator. All the guards had to do was look behind the towel. They never checked once." He rolled his blue eyes in disbelief. "They made it easy. All of the noise and commotion in jail helped too," he smiled.

Lewis related how he got through the fence, his rides, even calling his mother and wife. The fact that Frank already knew of the two toll calls helped verify Lewis' story.

Lewis estimated that he had access to $100,000 between April and September. He mentioned the expensive dental work, the purchase of two cars and a motorcycle, plus his new upscale suburban home with the attractive blonde companion. It was never clear whether the money was a gift or from Lewis' stashed assets.

Lewis bragged about being smart enough to stay away from Terry and the children. He knew that the house was being watched and told Frank that he had spotted the surveillance car the day he came by on his motorcycle.

They talked about the television show and Lewis said he would like to see it sometime. Several had called him about it. "When I heard about it," he laughed, "I considered going to the Bahamas or Mexico. I knew I would eventually be caught but I thought it would take longer. I never thought the show would be that effective."

The detective pursed his lips and shook his head. "I couldn't believe it myself. Just seven days after it was aired."

Many of these comments were repeated by Barnes when media people interviewed him later at the jail. Barnes began pleading his case to them. "I'm not a killer," he would say. "It just happened. Pete was a heroin addict and desperate to get some money. Pete shot the couple with their .22 gun."

He also told the media about his February jailhouse wedding and Alioto's part in it. Color photographs of Lewis, Terry, and their baby were in the local papers. Alioto and Sheriff Moreland downplayed the event as routine. There were many unfavorable responses to the marriage.

David Branum, Jr. objected. "Why should a killer like that be given any consideration whatsoever?"

Three days later a newspaper story fueled speculation that Barnes was aided in his escape. Local officials were still embarrassed by the escape and found it difficult to believe that he could escape and get to Texas without help. Lewis decided that if they wanted an accomplice, he'd damned well give them one. He called Frank to come to the jail.

Frank had already verified Lewis' escape story with the trustee by promising not to prosecute him. He believed Lewis. The entire sheriff's department had feared one of their guards had helped, and they gratefully embraced Frank's opinion. Now Frank was hearing the contrary.

Lewis reversed himself and told Alioto that he had been assisted by a guard who was paid $40,000. He said that just prior to his escape, the guard provided him with a crow bar and helped him later. Frank reluctantly recorded the new information, contacted the State Attorney's Office and FDLE.

An independent FDLE agent, John Burton, was assigned to investigate the charge. Lewis was vague about who paid the money to the guard. "Well, I just called up a friend of mine in Texas," he said.

"What number did you call and where did the meeting take place?" Burton asked.

"Well the guy just came and gave the guard the money," was his limp reply, "and that was the end of that. Never saw him again."

Lewis' story was weak and didn't stand scrutiny. The FDLE laboratory examined the window and said an iron bar, not a crow bar had been used. The accused guard was confronted, denied everything, and passed a polygraph test. It was concluded that he had nothing to do with the escape.

Barnes, however, refused to take a lie detector test. Much later he admitted to Frank that he had lied when he accused the guard. When asked why he had done this, Lewis replied, "I implicated him because he once told me that I deserved to die because those two people died. That's why. Because he thought I should go to the electric chair and he was holding me responsible for those people dying. I didn't like it and I decided to get him."

This closed the escape investigation. Barnes had pulled it off by himself.

◆

30

The double murder trial of Lewis Wesley Barnes finally began on Thursday, October 26, 1989, in Ocala, before Judge Victor Musleh. Assistant Public Defenders Trisha Jenkins and Bill Miller were now representing Barnes. Chief Assistant State Attorney Ric Ridgway was presenting the State's case. He had been rehired by the new State Attorney after the election.

Security precautions bordered on paranoia because of Barnes' well-known reputation. The decision was made to hold the hearing in the basement courtroom at the Marion County Jail.

The judge made a series of preliminary rulings in the case. He denied the defense request to suppress Barnes' confession after his initial arrest in Texas. His lawyers claimed that he gave statements to Smith and Alioto because they made him promises, that Barnes thought he would be testifying against two other men in the case not actually charged with the murders.

Judge Musleh refused to eliminate the death penalty as unconstitutional. He did rule some requests in Barnes' favor. A court reporter would record the trial and permission was granted to use a juror death penalty questionnaire. The jury selection was set for Wednesday, November 1st.

Ridgway was pleased. The confession was the centerpiece of his prosecution case and the death penalty was his announced goal. "I will seek the death penalty from beginning to end. We're going to be in court on the first, ready to try this case." he announced confidently.

Selection of the twelve-person jury never began. On Saturday, Barnes entered a plea agreement to avoid the risk of Florida's electric chair. Before Judge Musleh he pleaded no contest to two charges of first degree murder, armed robbery, trafficking in heroin, conspiracy to traffic in heroin, and escape.

The judge adjudicated Barnes guilty. He sentenced him to two life prison terms for murder and fifteen years for his escape from Marion County Jail. Barnes would serve a forty-year sentence in Texas first on attempted murder.

After the verdict, Ridgway said, "Barnes will die in jail." Barnes cried when he heard the sentencing. "My biggest regret is that I ever brought Pedro to Florida. He takes a lot of drugs and just went crazy." Barnes said he decided to plead guilty because he feared the electric chair. He didn't want to die in prison either, so he refused to testify against Covarrubias.

Ridgway had other plans. Since Pedro had a tentative parole date from federal prison in just fourteen months, and since he could not presently be prosecuted at the state level, Ridgway had himself appointed as a special federal prosecutor. Under federal jurisdiction he brought charges against Pedro for the interstate transport and sale of stolen Wayside antiques.

During this trial in federal court in Jacksonville, Florida, a procession of witnesses convicted Pedro. Marty Gates identified Pedro as having been in the store with Barnes. Julia placed Barnes and Pedro with the antiques in North Dakota. Norma Ferguson, owner and operator of the Las Vegas motel, identified Pedro as a resident there with Barnes. Finally, Ed Slade identified Pedro as being present at the sale of the antiques at the motel.

Pedro Covarrubias was convicted in April 1990, of the charges and sentenced to two consecutive ten year terms. This insured that he would stay in prison.

At this point, Lewis' wife and mother contacted Ridgway and Alioto. They wanted Lewis moved to a facility closer to them in Missouri, but authorities had no reason to help Lewis unless he was willing to testify against Pedro. Timing was good. Lewis could now bargain with less worry, so in September 1994, Barnes was brought back to Ocala to testify before the Marion County Grand Jury. The Grand Jury indicted Pedro Covarrubias for the Branum murders on the basis of his prior conviction on the transport and sale of the antiques and

Lewis Barnes' testimony.

Pedro pleaded no contest and was sentenced to fifty years in prison for killing the Branums.

"This is the functional equivalent of a life sentence." said Ridgway. "He won't be released before 2007 at age seventy-two."

The Covarrubias sentence was also closure for Alioto, who had retired in July. "This makes moving into retirement a lot easier."

Ridgway reflected that he knew of no other Marion County case as complex and broad in scope. Interpol, the FBI, Texas Rangers, and FDLE all had joined forces with the County Sheriff's Department. The FDLE highlighted the unique antiques and the FBI located them. The Las Vegas police helped break through the Barnes veil of aliases. The Texas Rangers captured Barnes twice. But it was Frank Alioto who kept gathering data and following every lead. Smith was an effective assistant, but the unwavering perseverance of Alioto as Task Force Chief led to the apprehension, double capture, and conviction of Barnes and Covarrubias.

"If there is a singular lesson from this case," pondered Ridgway, "it is that persistence pays off."

AFTERWORD

Officers Smith and Alioto were subpoenaed to testify in a corruption case against the FBI brought by the State of Nevada in 1990. Although they reluctantly testified, it was a bittersweet end to this bizarre case. The FBI would no longer intimidate local law enforcement.

Wayside Inn Antiques and Christmas Shop continues to be a successful business operated by family members at the same site. They are, understandably, reluctant to talk about that horrible night of robbery and homicide. However, those in the Ocala area who knew the victims, Betty and David Branum, still remember them well and sadly regret their senseless murders. Hopefully, this book will help prevent similar tragedies or inspire further outstanding law enforcement efforts.

ORDER FORM

Yes, I'd like to order additional copies of *Murder at Wayside Antiques*.

QUAN		PRICE	TOTAL
	MURDER AT WAYSIDE ANTIQUES	$12.95	
	Florida Residents please add	6%	
	Shipping & Handling	see below	
TOTAL			$

Shipping & Handling
Please allow 3-4 weeks for delivery

QUAN	AMOUNT	ADD S&H
1	$ 12.95	$ 3.00
2	25.90	4.00
3	38.85	6.00
4-7	51.80-90.65	10.00
8-10	103.60-129.50	15.00

MAKE A COPY, FILL OUT, AND
MAIL WITH PAYMENT TO:

Raven Press, Inc.
P.O. Box 410368
Melbourne, Florida 32941-0368

☐ Check or Money Order enclosed   Payable to Raven Press, Inc.

☐ MC   # _____

☐ VISA   Sig _____

daytime phone _____ exp date _____

For quantity discounts contact us by mail at the above address or E-mail us at RavenP_Inc@aol.com

---

SHIP TO: PLEASE PRINT

Name _____

Address _____

City _____ Zip _____